THE BOOK OF THE SNOW
LE LIVRE DE LA NEIGE

François Jacqmin
THE BOOK OF THE SNOW
LE LIVRE DE LA NEIGE

LE LIVRE DE LA NEIGE

❧

Translated by Philip Mosley
Introduced by Clive Scott

Arc
PUBLICATIONS
2010

Published by Arc Publications,
Nanholme Mill, Shaw Wood Road
Todmorden OL14 6DA, UK

Original poems copyright © Editions de la Différence 1990
Translation copyright © Philip Mosley 2010
Introduction copyright © Clive Scott 2010

Design by Tony Ward
Printed by Lightning Source

978 1904614 55 5 (pbk)
978 1906570 02 6 (hbk)

ACKNOWLEDGEMENTS
Arc Publications thank Editions de la Différence,
publishers of François Jacqmin's *Le Livre de la neige*,
for granting permission to reproduce the original French text as
part of this bi-lingual edition.

Cover painting:
Old Orchard in Winter (1925) by Valerius de Saedeleer,
courtesy of Mr. Henry Simon

Supported by
ARTS COUNCIL
ENGLAND

Arc Publications 'Visible Poets' series
Editor: Jean Boase-Beier

To Frans De Haes and
Monique De Plaen

CONTENTS

Series Editor's Note / 11
Translator's Preface / 13
Introduction / 17

26 / La neige… • Snow… / 27
26 / Vient le temps… • The time comes… / 27
28 / Pour rendre… • To return… / 29
28 / Le paysage est arrêté • The landscape is fixed / 29
30 / Lorsqu'on suit… • When we follow… / 31
30 / Les personnes bien • Gentlefolk… / 31
élevées…
32 / Ce qu'on entend… • What you hear… / 33
32 / Traquée par la nuit… • Hounded by the night… / 33
34 / Je ferme les yeux • I close my eyes / 35
34 / Si nous avons… • If we have… / 35
36 / En poésie… • In poetry… / 37
36 / On lève les yeux… • We raise our eyes… / 37
38 / Pendant un instant • For an inexhaustible
inépuisable… instant… / 39
38 / Les cerises sont serrées… • The cherries are packed / 39
tight…

40 / La nuit… • Night… / 41
40 / Le brouillard… • The fog… / 41
42 / On soupçonne… • You suspect… / 43
42 / Nul ne passe avec • No one gets by with
sa parole his speech / 43
44 / La neige est partout… • The snow is everywhere… / 45
44 / Celui qui vit… • He who lives… / 45
46 / Figée dans sa crypte • Frozen in its icy crypt… / 47
de glace…

46 / Il est minuit… • It is midnight… / 47

48 / Notre délabrement… • My ruin… / 49

48 / Je me réjouis… • I am delighted… / 49

50 / Ce n'est pas la justesse… • It is not the aptness… / 51

50 / Quand l'âme… • When the soul… / 51

52 / La nuit est vieille… • Night is old… / 53

52 / Tout à coup… • All of a sudden… / 53

54 / Il doit se trouver • There has to be
une médisance adroite… a handy slander… / 55

54 / Qui déchiffrera… • Who will make sense of… / 55

56 / Le rôle… • The role… / 57

56 / L'exercice des lettres… • Literary practice… / 57

58 / Belle… • Beautiful… / 59

58 / Tête baissée… • Heads lowered… / 59

60 / Nous comprîmes que… • We understood that… / 61

60 / Il n'est rien de si • There is nothing as
fade… pointless… / 61

62/ Que peut-on espérer… • What hope is there… / 63

62 / Elle ne se rendait • The snow was going
en aucun lieu… nowhere… / 63

64 / L'inclination… • The tendency… / 65

64 / On commence un vers… • We begin a verse… / 65

66 / Lorsque la neige • When the snow
cessa de tomber… stopped falling… / 67

66 / A force de… • By dint of… / 67

68 / Quelle leçon… • What lesson… / 69

68 / La détresse rectiligne… • The rectilinear distress… / 69

70 / Celui qui eut une seule • He who had a single
pensée claire… clear thought… / 71

70 / Parfois, dans la nuit… • Sometimes, in the night… / 71

72 / La fontaine… • The fountain… / 73

72 / Sous la neige… • Beneath the snow… / 73

74 / Là où tombe la neige… • Where the snow falls… / 75

74 / L'être se détache • Being detaches itself
de la nuit… from the night… / 75

76 / Les petits tableaux… • The small scenes… / 77

76 / Touché… • Moved… / 77

78 / L'immense est scellé… • The boundless is sealed… / 79

78 / Le mât du néant… • The mast of nothingness… / 79

80 / Je ne tolère plus… • I no longer stand… / 81

80 / D'aucuns utilisent • Some use the sled… / 81
le traîneau…

82 / Vous souffrez un peu… • You suffer a little… / 83

82 / Celui qui écoute… • He who listens… / 83

84 / Le rien m'étouffe aussi… • Nothing stifles me too… / 85

84 / Nous attendons… • We await… / 85

86 / Je traverse l'émail… • I cross the enamel… / 87

86 / Ce n'est pas mourir… • It is not dying… / 87

88 / Il est des hommes… • There are men… / 89

88 / On ouvre le livre… • I open the book… / 89

90 / L'être… • Being… / 91

90 / Ce à quoi tout est • That to which all is
donné… given… / 91

92 / La nuit abuse… • Night exploits… / 93

92 / La nostalgie… • Nostalgia… / 93

94 / Seuls les séraphins • Only the dimwitted
obtus… seraphim… / 95

94 / La seule chose… • The only thing… / 95

96 / Nous ne pouvons • We cannot carry on… / 97
continuer…

96 / Ne parlons plus … • Let us talk no more… / 97

98 / Dans le cliquetis… • In the clinking… / 99

98 / Une bise féroce… • A ferocious blast… / 99

100 / Nous avons dépassé… • We have gone beyond… / 101

100 / La contradiction… • The contradiction… / 101

102 / On ne voit rien… • We see nothing… / 103

102 / Une première chute • A first snowfall… / 103
de neige…

104 / Vient l'époque… • There comes an age… / 105

104 / Il ne reste plus rien… • There is nothing left… / 105

106 / La neige s'approchait… • The snow came close… / 107

106 / Le repos des sapins… • The repose of firs… / 107

108 / Lorsque je ne vis • When I no longer saw
plus rien… anything… / 109

108 / Il est perspicace… • Perceptive is he… / 109

110 / Les ailes basses • The forest's low wings… / 111
de la forêt…

110 / Dans la vocifération • In the white clamour… / 111
blanche…

112 / Toute chose démontrée… • Everything proven… / 113

112 / Puisque le silence… • Since silence… / 113

114 / Le soir descend… • Evening draws in… / 115

114 / Je ne puis plus… • I can no longer… / 115

116 / L'impossible… • The impossible… / 117

116 / Fort… • With the snow… / 117

118 / Nous conjuguons… • We conjugate… / 119

118 / Ce qui commence… • What begins… / 119

120 / Il n'y avait aucun • There was no land-
repère… mark… / 121

120 / Il est éloquent… • It is eloquent… / 121

122 / L'être incline… • Being tilts… / 123

122 / Il n'y a ni forêt ni • There is neither forest nor
contemplation… thought… / 123

124 / La lune a révélé… • The moon has revealed… / 125

124 / Après qu'il eut neigé… • After it had snowed… / 125

126 / Il y eut quelques • There were several
instants… moments… / 127

126 / Je me fais rare… • I make myself scarce… / 127

128 / Le bruit… • The noise… / 129

128 / Nous ne sommes • I am not an author… / 129
pas un auteur…

130 / Le froid consumait… • Cold consumed… / 131

130 / Depuis que le gel… • Since the frost… / 131

132 / J'ai dû rassembler… • I have had to muster… / 133

132 / Je n'atteins plus • I do not connect with
le monde… the world anymore… / 133

134 /Il ne suffit pas… • It is not enough… / 135

134 / La fin du jour… • Day's end… / 135

136 / Que serait ce • What would be that
triomphe… triumph… / 137

136 / Au début du soir… • In early evening… / 137

Biographical Notes / 138

SERIES EDITOR'S NOTE

The 'Visible Poets' series was established in 2000, and set out to challenge the view that translated poetry could or should be read without regard to the process of translation it had undergone. Since then, things have moved on. Today there is more translated poetry available and more debate on its nature, its status, and its relation to its original. We know that translated poetry is neither English poetry that has mysteriously arisen from a hidden foreign source, nor is it foreign poetry that has silently rewritten itself in English. We are more aware that translation lies at the heart of all our cultural exchange; without it, we must remain artistically and intellectually insular.

One of the aims of the series was, and still is, to enrich our poetry with the very best work that has appeared elsewhere in the world. And the poetry-reading public is now more aware than it was at the start of this century that translation cannot simply be done by anyone with two languages. The translation of poetry is a creative act, and translated poetry stands or falls on the strength of the poet-translator's art. For this reason 'Visible Poets' publishes only the work of the best translators, and gives each of them space, in a Preface, to talk about the trials and pleasures of their work.

From the start, 'Visible Poets' books have been bilingual. Many readers will not speak the languages of the original poetry but they, too, are invited to compare the look and shape of the English poems with the originals. Those who can are encouraged to read both. Translation and original are presented side-by-side because translations do not displace the originals; they shed new light on them and are in turn themselves illuminated by the presence of their source poems. By drawing the readers' attention to the act of translation itself, it is the aim of these books to make the work of both the original poets and their translators more visible.

Jean Boase-Beier

TRANSLATOR'S PREFACE

A BEAUTIFUL DISORIENTATION: LOST IN (THE BOOK OF) THE SNOW

An avowedly reluctant poet, François Jacqmin writes poetry for all that. Like Rieux in Camus's *The Plague*, if less redemptory, he ultimately opts to put pen to paper "pour ne pas être de ceux qui se taisent" (so as not to be one of those who stay silent). Sceptical of art, language, and the intellect to the point of near defeatism, Jacqmin is nonetheless a poet who enjoys, as one of his lines has it, "the dubious felicity of expression". He not only continues to write but does so in a manner suggestive of a dedicated and skilful craftsman at work. Having retreated far from the madding crowd, especially the charivari of literary culture, Jacqmin, an admirer of the Stoics, realizes Marcus Aurelius's unfulfilled dream of composing aphorisms in rural quietude. In the 107 *dizains* (ten-line poems) plus three nine-liners and two eleven-liners that comprise the 112 poems in *The Book of the Snow*, the poet meditates on being, on nothingness, on perception, on art, and on the vanity of human wishes.

Jacqmin finds his metaphors in a bleak and beautiful natural landscape, one ever shifting while seemingly still, one ever under illusion and erasure while reassuringly *there*. The snow-covered scene suggests an indistinct space, yet it is anything but that: our senses reel, we can no longer formulate, "we have gone beyond meaning", as he puts it. Cruelly sardonic, he contrasts our empty dreams with a vision of nature as a place of fullness, a place stripped of any affective, sentimental, or picturesque elements. Here the poet may perhaps tap into a measure, albeit small, of transcendent truth.

In translating *The Book of the Snow* as *visible* poetry, I have sought a tonal balance between the poet's serious and lighthearted sides. His irreverent attitude bears traces of his early flirtation with the neo-surrealist Phantomas group. We may discern some serious debunking going on in these poems, and they deserve to be read as such. Jacqmin, a subtle purveyor of gallows humour, invites us to join in his aesthetic end game, rather as Beckett's eponymous narrator in *The Unnamable* concludes, "where I am, I don't know, I'll never know, in the silence you don't know, you must go on, I can't go on, I'll go on". Whatever *is* serious, even profound, on the level of philosophical enquiry in *The Book of the Snow* is not methodically expressed. Such intellectual pretension would be anathema to Jacqmin, who claimed anyway to have abandoned his former interest in ontology. His method is poetic, his tone is lyrical, and his strategies are irony, allusion, and paradox. He harnesses tautological statements to the measure of his verse. If knowledge, wisdom, and insight happen to follow, they do so in visionary fragments, often barely perceptible or distinguishable, like objects faintly made out in the all encompassing snow.

As the snow falls, Jacqmin's irony suffuses it. By evoking whiteness and purity, dis-solution, dis-appearance, de-formation, he invents a Mallarméan palimpsest, a suite of poems aspiring to perfection, present yet absent in the pristine, silent, snowy spaces of the page. He enjoys his amiable duplicity, demonstrating a refined poetic art while simultaneously deriding its futile aims and the language that constructs it. He also enjoys offering us his eloquent French, revelling in its Latinisms and an occasional long sweep of its line, while confessing nonetheless to an anti-Jacobinism, to a greater ease with the English words in which he first started to write poetry than with the lofty and essentialist ring of his native tongue.

This preference on the part of the poet might offer the translator a broad licence to anglicise metre, diction, and line. Conventional translation practice would support such a move. But Jacqmin is to be a *visible* poet; thus, I have retained his stanza, line, and word as far as possible without losing too much shape and pulse in the target language. I have also sought to convey his avoidance of any narrative or logical sequence, though typically an illusion of these elements exists to give a semblance of structure to the volume as a whole. Rather, as we might expect, a crosscurrent of themes and motifs flows within individual poems, among groups of them, and throughout the book.

Many thanks are due to Jean Boase-Beier, editor of this series, for her patient encouragement of this translation, and to Arc for finding a place for it among renderings of other "Visible Poets"; to Clive Scott, himself an innovative translator of French poetry, for kindly writing an introduction; to Catherine Daems, at the Archives and Museum of Literature in Brussels, for bringing her expert knowledge of Jacqmin's work to bear on a careful and helpful reading of my text, and for making many valuable suggestions; to Henry Simon for generously permitting use of Valerius de Saedeleer's snowscape for the cover art of this book; and to Editions de la Différence, publisher of the original text in 1990, for granting permission to publish this work.

Philip Mosley

INTRODUCTION

François Jacqmin is a poet ill at ease with his poetry. Where others find in writing an antidote to the cares of existence, for Jacqmin it is only the invalid's bedside companion.[1] Where other writers find in poetry a privileged mode of access to Being, or the transcendent, or expanded consciousness, for Jacqmin it is a troublesome medium, obstructive, frustrating, of uncertain legitimacy. And at the root of this writerly unease lies his sense of being a linguistic orphan, without a 'native' language.

Jacqmin and his parents took refuge in England in 1940 – Jacqmin was ten years old – where he learned English and immersed himself in English literature. He wrote poetry in English between the ages of thirteen and twenty-one. And when he returned to Belgium in 1948, he recovered a French which he never felt quite at home with: "Mon absence d'attachement à l'égard du français devait être renforcée par cette constatation que je fis à son sujet, à savoir, la pauvreté de ses moyens poétiques" (My lack of attachment to French must have been reinforced by what I observed about it, namely, the poverty of its poetic means).[2] Elsewhere he expresses the view that, for Walloons, French is not the appropriate language, that they still have their true language to find.[3] Sometimes English seems to be the only tolerable language of communication.[4] But Jacqmin's restless discomfort with inher-

---

[1] See François Jacqmin, *Le Poème exacerbé* (Louvain-la-Neuve: Presses Universitaires de Louvain, 1992), p. 33. *Le Poème exacerbé* is a sequence of passages in which Jacqmin explores his literary beginnings, his uneasy relationship with philosophical thought and his habits of composition, constructs a poetics (as best he can), and presents his principal volumes of verse.

[2] *ibid.*, p. 18

[3] See François Jacqmin, 'Journal des *Nuits d'Hiver*', *Balises*, 3/4, 2002/3, p. 162 *Le Livre de la neige* was originally to have been entitled *Les Nuits d'hiver*, but during the correction of proofs, Jacqmin was prevailed upon by Alain Bosquet to re-think the title.

[4] *ibid.*, p. 169

ited languages is a symptom of a larger discomfort with the inheritance of language itself.

In one sense, Jacqmin faces a Mallarméan predicament: language trespasses on a white page which, like snow, creates a space of pure potentiality, of origins yet to be realized, where all is still intact. Language forces us to adopt an identity, to re-assume the burden of memory, to think potentiality into something else, something already with a place and function, to destroy the indeterminate, to confront our own uncertainty. If Jacqmin looks to inhabit the featureless landscapes of desert and snow, it is because of his wish to be utterly dispossessed of the interfering paraphernalia of definition, differentiation, arrangement, conclusion. But if the white expanse of page, or snow, promises a state of pre-linguistic "émerveillement" (wonderment), it also tempts us with the promise, through the very process of writing, of a post-linguistic return to the pre-linguistic. What if language, at first experienced as an intruder, trespassing on blank space, could achieve its own eradication by conjuring up the very silence which its voice insists on breaking? Jacqmin tells us: "On ne peut regarder l'œuvre d'art que sous l'angle d'un désir de reconquête d'une inspiration perdue, d'une carence qui nous comblait. L'œuvre ne gagne que par ce qu'elle permet en deçà d'elle-même" (One can view the work of art only from the angle of a desire to reconquer a lost inspiration, a lack which fulfilled us. The work succeeds only to the degree that it allows what is anterior to it).[5]

Language reaches for reality, but by its very nature can only mediate the real, can only *intervene between* perception and reality and thus seem to drive them further apart. The knowledge, the consciousness of self, that language produces, breaks the spell of simple being. Language cannot penetrate the world's opacity; it can only expect to compound that opacity through its own ambivalences and approximations. Unfinishedness thus becomes

[5] *op. cit.*, 1992, p. 120

16

a vital safeguard against any illusions of success, any falling back into lazy complacency. If Jacqmin writes one hundred and twelve *dizains*, it is because the experiment of utterance must be tried again and again, and must repeatedly be allowed to fail; this is not a *cycle* of poems and all that that implies of satisfying fulfilment; this is an obsessive and unending return to the workbench. And the absence of titles for his poems suggests two things: first, that his poems can never achieve the status, the confidence, the substantiality, of the entitled; and secondly, that the reader cannot fall back on any easy key or clue to a poem's preoccupations, but must find his / her own way through the process of sense-making.

With the coming of the snow is the promise of the recovery of re-potentiated language:

> À onze heures du matin, il se mit à neiger. À ce moment retentit la voix des enfants de l'école maternelle proche d'ici. L'effet de la neige sembla être magique. Car tout-à-coup, et à l'unisson, ces petits enfants se mirent à scander 'il nei-ge, il nei-ge' et ce fut peut-être un des moments où le mot, ou plutôt le cri, fut au plus près de la chose. Leurs cris retentissaient naturellement, et avait la blancheur et l'allure même de la neige.'

> (At eleven o'clock in the morning, it began to snow. Simultaneously, the voices of the children of the nearby nursery school rang out. The effect of the snow seemed to be magical. Because suddenly, and in unison, these young children began to chant 'it's sno-owing, it's sno-owing' and it was perhaps one of those moments when language, or rather the cry, came closest to what it named. Their cries echoed naturally, and had the whiteness and the very motion of the snow).[6]

To achieve this near-coincidence with the phenomena of the world, three things are necessary:

---

[6] *op. cit.*, 2002 / 3, p. 162

17

(a) the attitude of the child: "Je ne cherche pas à comprendre; je demeure perpétuellement au stade infantile de l'étonnement" (I do not try to understand; I remain perpetually in the childlike condition of astonishment).[7] Jacqmin's privileging of the childlike has much in common with Baudelaire's affiliation of the child with the convalescent and the genius, in their shared ability to endow even the trivial with intensified being, with the vividness of the new; Baudelaire speaks of the "œil fixe et animalement extatique des enfants devant le *nouveau*" (staring and animally ecstatic eyes of children when faced with the *new*).[8] Jacqmin may share, unwillingly, Baudelaire's view that the childlike must, in order to express itself, be supplemented by adult faculties and "l'esprit analytique" (analytical spirit), but his ideal of response is a pre-expressive, pre-poetic one.[9] From time to time, Jacqmin looks forward to the day when he will have done with writing, when he can re-dedicate himself "au sujet que connaît l'enfance, c'est-à-dire, au rien naturel" (to the subject known to children, that is to say, to the natural any-old-thing).[10]

(b) relatedly, the evaporation of the self, a release from the strait-jacket of self-preoccupation, of intellectual tics. This compulsion also reveals a Baudelairian kinship. What Baudelaire identifies as the "vaporisation [...] du *Moi*"[11] entails a total sensory

---

[7] *op. cit.,* 1992, p. 58

[8] Charles Baudelaire, *Œuvres complètes II*, edited by Claude Pichois (Paris : Gallimard, 1976), p. 690

[9] "Au cours de cette petite promenade, il me vient une impression assez faible, mais subtile et réelle. En regardant le sentier si agréable et doux à la marche, il me vient une impression d'enfance, une impression d'avant la poésie" (In the course of this short walk, I am visited by an impression, not very strong, but subtle and real enough. As I look at the path, so pleasant and congenial for walking along, I am struck by a childhood impression, an impression prior to poetry). See *op. cit.,* 2002 / 3, p. 167

[10] *ibid.,* p. 168

[11] Charles Baudelaire, *Œuvres complètes I*, edited by Claude Pichois (Paris : Gallimard, 1975), p. 676

18

availability to all phenomena, an empathic transferability of consciousness; Baudelaire calls it: "cette sainte prostitution de l'âme qui se donne tout entière, poésie et charité,[12] à l'imprévu qui se montre, à l'inconnu qui passe" (this sacred prostitution of the soul which gives itself, entire, poetry and charity, to the unforeseen that appears, to the unknown that passes by).[13] And for Jacqmin, as for Baudelaire, the achievement of self-evaporation brings with it an apparent expansion of space, extending perceptual capacity (poem 13, "Pendant un instant inépuisable… / For an inexhaustible instant…", pp. 38 / 9). Jacqmin must, as it were, live the dissolution of his thought, with its arguments and continuities and objectives, and live in the inchoate mass of things. The position that the poet adopts is as near to self-effacement as can be achieved without ceasing to write. Schoenaers points out that this process of self-dispossession is favoured by certain conditions, by nightfall (poems 110 "Le fin du jour… / Day's end…", pp. 134 / 5, and 112 "Au début du soir… / In early evening…", pp. 136 / 7), by walking (see footnote 9), by staying at home (poem 6 "Les personnes bien élevées se tiennent chez elles… / Gentlefolk stay at home…", pp. 30 / 1),[14] and, we might add, by desert and snow. Once this state is achieved, barriers between self and non-self, between objects, between subject and object, between inside and outside, dissolve, as if beneath a blanket of snow (poem 48 "Sous la neige… / Beneath the snow…", pp. 72 / 3, poem 77 "On ne voit rien… / We see nothing…", pp. 102 / 3, and poem 78 "Une première chute… / At first

---

[12] The notion of 'charity', in this connection, comes with equal naturalness to Jacqmin's pen: "Et sans doute cette impression d'avant la naissance du poème était-elle plus profondément 'charitable' à mon égard" (And doubtless this impression prior to the birth of the poem was more deeply 'charitable' in regard to me). See *op. cit.,* 2002 /3, pp.167-8.
[13] *op. cit.,* 1975, p. 291
[14] Christian Schoenaers, *Références : Études littéraires (Poulet, Jacqmin, de Duve)* (Brussels : Christian Schoenaers, 1998), pp. 68-70

snowfall...", pp. 102 / 3); we experience the transferability of consciousness, yes, but also the permeability of things and their reflexivity: things look back at us (poem 33 "Belle... / Beautiful...", pp. 58 / 9: "Watching it [the snow], the soul knew it was being watched"); and the trivial assumes a seemingly inexhaustible plenitude: "Je n'aurai pas assez de mes jours pour explorer les mystères d'un potager, pour expliquer l'insondable enigma d'une jardinière que l'on accroche à son balcon" (I will not have life-time enough to explore the mysteries of a vegetable patch, nor to explain the fathomless enigma of a jardinière that is hung on a balcony).[15] The less the poet intrudes, the more, correspondingly, the banal phenomenon is sufficient to itself, the more existential density it acquires.

Jacqmin freely admits to the tautological turn of his writing;[16] this is to favour the given over the created, to cultivate a condition in which nothing is invented, but nothing is undone; it is the excursion which brings a return home. Those who have ambitions beyond the given, like the traveler, find that they are chasing a receding horizon, or, like the thinker, that the area of their ignorance is correspondingly increasing.[17] In this sense, Jacqmin's poems make no progress. But in tautological relationships, the same need not live in an inertial state with itself (x is x); it may assume 'argumentative' forms, conditional, say (if x, then x), or causal (because x, therefore x), or concessive (although x, x). These structures generate a certain energy within tautology, a certain dynamic of perception. Tautology is an attempt, not to affirm, but to capture, to embody, the irreducibility of things.

(c) a language whose *material / physical* kinship with event has not been diverted, obscured by meaning. This language is a language as if *within* the French that leaves Jacqmin disconcerted,

---

[15] *op. cit.*, 1992, p. 57

[16] *ibid.*, p. 78. See also Sabrina Parent, '*Le Livre de la neige* de François Jacqmin : Poésie et tautologie', *Balises*, 3/4, 2002/3, pp. 139-60

[17] *op. cit.*, 1992, p. 77

is the lost Walloon, is something half-concealed in the folds and nuances of the language he writes. But if language acts as a barrier to the seizure of our surroundings, how is its obstructiveness to be minimized? First, by outwitting it with poetry: "A la recherche d'angles de vue inédits, j'entends suspendre les conventions de l'esprit analytique. [...] En réalité, nous ne voulons pas comprendre, nous voulons surprendre notre pensée, l'indigner, s'il le faut, par des insinuations poétiques" (In search of new angles of vision, I mean to suspend the conventions of the analytical spirit. [...] In reality, we do not wish to understand, but to surprise our thought, to provoke it to indignation, if need be, by poetic insinuations).[18] Secondly, by the effort to "réduire mes vers à leur plus simple expression" (to reduce my verse to its simplest expression).[19] Rhetoric must be thrust away – and, in this respect, Jacqmin marks his distance from Baudelaire – because it is beset by expressive self-satisfaction, by egotism.[20] The hand that can hold the snow is the hand which has a zero temperature; nothing must occlude "une poésie plus fermement enracinée dans la totalité des choses" (a poetry more firmly rooted in the totality of things).[21]

All these are essential moves towards the recovery of origins, origins of being, pre-egoist, pre-literate, pre-rational, unformed. But any success is temporary, on sufferance, or merely glimpsed. The founding premise is always failure: "Nous tenons ce que nous faisons pour une abdication. Ainsi, l'art, le verbe sont des concessions que le silence de l'âme ne cautionnera jamais. L'âme ne parle pas" (We consider what we do an abdication. Thus, art, the word, are concessions that the silence of the soul will never assent to. The soul does not speak).[22] If snow had used

[18] *ibid.,* p. 41
[19] *ibid.,* p. 41
[20] *ibid.,* p. 10
[21] *op. cit.,* 2002 / 3, p. 161
[22] *op. cit.,* 1992, p. 90

language, it would not yet have managed to be white (poem 88 "Puisque le silence... / Since silence...", pp. 112 / 3).

Jacqmin is a philosopher-poet, but one for whom thought itself may be a dangerous distraction, may monopolise the mind, may never free one from the interrogative, or may capitulate too easily to the temptations of the abstract and the absolute. But it is a turn of mind which gives his work an ethical rigour. It makes a virtue of finding no easy answers. Indeed, we must learn to refuse knowledge, which is an instrument of oppression.[23] And it is the obliterating whiteness of the snow, "l'extase blanche" (the white ecstasy),[24] which protects Jacqmin from the lure of knowledge, from the *interpretative* functions of perception.

We are accustomed to the philosopher as aphorist (e.g. Nietzsche, Wittgenstein), and Jacqmin acknowledges his own devotion to the aphorism: "Je suis quelqu'un d'obsédé par l'aphorisme, j'ai toujours pratiqué ça" (I am someone obsessed by aphorisms, I have always written them).[25] But the aphoristic turn of Jacqmin's utterances has an ambiguous effect: "We no longer manage / to be unknowing enough of our own needs " (poem 16 "Le brouillard a élevé... / The fog has lifted...", pp. 40 / 1). What we think might be a privileged insight turns out to sound more like a rebus; what seems like a confident compression of summarising thought turns out to be the beginning of relativity and fluid thinking. No aphorism is adequate to its purpose; one aphorism always necessitates another. And the aphorism seems to hang between the unauthored and the authored: its lapidary nature invests it with a certain impersonality, but one feels, too, the pressures of an individual consciousness looking for its way.

Another way of viewing this aphoristic tendency is as a habit of parataxis, the use of a syntax which eschews complex conjunc-

---

[23] *ibid.,* p. 72
[24] *ibid.,* p. 72
[25] Pierre-Yves Soucy, 'L'Incertitude à l'œuvre', *Textyles*, 13 (pp. 13-26), 1996, p. 21

tional relationships, a syntax of consecutive main clauses. What parataxis puts at risk is textual cohesiveness, the overt connections between one sentence and the next. Gaps may seem to occur in the fabric of argument or narrative, gaps that seem to derive from uncertainty or ignorance, gaps that the reader must seek to fill. But getting the world to hang together, getting things intimately to relate to each other, trying to understand the invisible weave of motive and reason, the mysteries of being, is precisely what Jacqmin's poetry is about.

Correspondingly, Jacqmin's *dizain* itself looks rather like an accidental form. By virtue of being returned to the left-hand margin, rather than indented, the line-overflow becomes itself a line of verse. And yet, clearly, some lines are split for reasons other than overflow, by their urgent but impenetrable need to be autonomous lines of verse. On the other hand, the lines seem to have no metrico-rhythmic *raison d'être*. And yet, of course, everything creates a rhythm, a rhythm of utterance which is a rhythm of attention, which is a set of fluctuations of consciousness, which is feeling one's way towards and through an appropriate syntax. No rhythm recurs, no rhythm is derived from a previous mould, no rhythm acts as a template for future rhythms: this is a world in constant psychic and perceptual metamorphosis, a world in which nothing wants to exist for long, is elusive, on the point of disappearance. And yet the *dizain* is a species of fixed form, a form which perhaps ironically alludes to the expressive ambitions of the classic ten-line stanza of the French grand ode, a frame for circumscribing and focussing: the *dizain* is Jacqmin's fixed horizon, that keeps him in his own here and now, and prevents him wandering into chimerical distances.

Jacqmin, we might say, is the poet of contradictions: "Il ne m'a pas été donné de m'abriter derrière une conviction précise tant mes divisions furent constantes et puissantes. C'est cela qui a déterminé le fond de ma poésie. L'horreur, mais aussi l'extase, ont à jamais mêlé leurs eaux en moi" (It has not been given to me to find shelter behind a particular conviction, so powerful and unremitting were my inner divisions. That is what has given a determining shape to the ground of my poetry. Horror, but ecstasy too, have for ever mingled their waters in me).[26] In the last sentence here, we again hear reference to a Baudelairian condition. But, however wearying these contradictions are, they give substance to Jacqmin's existence.[27] And, sometimes, contradictions achieve a fragile equilibrium, an ability to exist more or less peacefully, in paradox : Jacqmin's *dizains*, for example, are fixed forms remarkable for their flexibility, a prose that persuades itself into poetry, a poetry which, as he says of the snow, 'had the light tone of depth' (poem 38 "Elle ne se rendait en aucun lieu... / The snow was going nowhere...", pp. 62 / 3); more particularly, the language that positively prevents the achievement of access, can, for all that, take us to the threshold of access. We are now able to enjoy this poignant but elevating predicament in Philip Mosley's sensitive and engaging translation.

Clive Scott

[26] *op. cit.*, 1992, p. 57
[27] *ibid.*, p. 58

THE BOOK OF THE SNOW
LE LIVRE DE LA NEIGE

¶

La neige
se couche sur la neige et annule sa blancheur.
Tout s'établit et s'éteint
comme cela.
L'être est ménager; il règle d'un seul
trait
la bourrasque ou la propension au pourquoi.
La certitude originelle se maintient
ainsi,
en ne distinguant rien de rien.

¶

Vient le temps où l'hésitation se révèle la manière
la plus pragmatique d'être au monde.
On regarde la dissolution
de la vérité et de la matière
sans émotion. La musique est jugée diffamante
dès les premières mesures.
On ne s'affaire plus autour de l'absolu; on
le considère comme une
mélancolie déplacée,
une inconvenance de la tristesse.

¶

Snow
overlays snow and cancels out its whiteness.
Everything lives and dies out
like that.
Being keeps house; at a stroke it
settles
the squall or the propensity to reason why.
Original certainty remains
thus,
by distinguishing nothing from nothing.

¶

The time comes when hesitation reveals itself
as the most practical way of being in the world.
You watch the dissolution
of truth and matter
without emotion. Music is deemed slanderous
from the very first bars.
You no longer fuss over the absolute; you
consider it to be a
displaced melancholy,
an improper sadness.

¶

Pour rendre son poids au peuplier,
il faudrait
que je repousse la figure convulsée du récit.
Pour accomplir
une œuvre littéraire,
il me faudrait évincer le temps du compte rendu
sans
exaspérer le reste.
En attendant,
tout m'est impossible et le verbe en abuse.

¶

Le paysage est arrêté. Il est cet attelage
poudreux
qui s'enlise dans sa blancheur.
Ses essieux
s'enfoncent dans l'innocence despotique
de la neige.
Sans être égarés, nous commençons à redouter
le nulle part, et surtout
ce silence inclément
qui tonne contre l'affront de tout voyage.

¶

To return to the poplar its weight,
I would have to
reject narrative's convulsed form.
To accomplish
a literary work,
I would have to oust the stage of review
without
worsening the rest of it.
Meanwhile,
all is impossible to me and language exploits the fact.

¶

The landscape is fixed. It is that powdery
yoke
which bogs down in its whiteness.
Its axles
sink deep in the despotic innocence
of the snow.
Though not quite lost, we start to dread
nowhere, and especially
that inclement silence
which thunders against the affront of all travel.

¶

Lorsqu'on suit la pente d'un argument jusqu'à
sa preuve,
on s'aperçoit qu'il n'y a rien à soutenir.
Ne sachant pas que le mot
engendre plus de distance que l'espace,
d'aucuns se sont résolus à parler comme on se met
en chemin
par un temps noir de bise. On les a retrouvés
morts
dans la poussière blanche de la signification.

¶

Les personnes bien élevées se tiennent chez elles.
Le voyage
révèle ce que l'âme a de lamentable.
Aller ailleurs, c'est
découdre
la fronce d'innocence que l'innocence tisse
autour de notre lieu.
C'est la raison pour laquelle je tiens à rester
dans mes meubles:
ils sont mes absolus usuels et déchirants.

¶

When we follow the slope of an argument right down to
its proof,
we realize there is nothing to uphold.
Not knowing that the word
engenders more distance than does space,
some have resolved to speak as if starting
on their way
under a black northern sky. We found them
dead
in the white dust of meaning.

¶

Gentlefolk stay at home.
Travel
reveals what is lamentable in the soul.
To go elsewhere is to
unstitch
the gather of innocence which innocence weaves
around our place.
It is the reason why I set great store on staying
at home amid my own things:
they are my common heartrending absolute.

¶

Ce qu'on entend lorsque l'âme
se recueille
n'a rien du triomphe insolent de la musique.
C'est un chœur
affable et flou qui, par la bouche de l'incertain,
acclame les relevailles de l'infini.
C'est la suprême
économie de l'écoute qui est requise pour saisir
ce que chuchote la blancheur
après la dernière ligne d'un poème.

¶

Traquée par la nuit, la neige poussa la porte,
et avança jusqu'au cœur du logis.
Elle pénétrait
comme ces convictions douces que l'on a
en rêvant.
Puis, elle s'est assise au milieu de l'âtre.
Installée dans le giron des flammes,
elle contemplait
mes songes. Elle était lasse de sa blancheur,
et attendait mon ombre compatissante.

¶

What you hear when the soul
reflects
has none of music's insolent triumph.
It is an affable and muffled choir
which, from the mouth of the uncertain,
acclaims the churching of infinity.
A supreme
economy of hearing is required to grasp
what whiteness whispers
after a poem's last line.

¶

Hounded by the night, the snow pushed the door
and advanced to the heart of the abode.
It penetrated
like those gentle convictions you have
in dreams.
Then it sat down in the middle of the hearth.
Installed in the fold of the flames,
it contemplated
my thoughts. It was tired of its whiteness,
and awaited my compassionate shadow.

¶

Je ferme les yeux,
et les mélèzes entrent dans une phase ascétique.
Je tremble,
et mon corps devient une appréhension plutôt
que le lieu d'un frisson.
Je m'amenuise
jusqu'à l'ivoire de l'ellipse.
Il a fallu que l'infini se rapproche de moi
pour que je ne découvre rien. C'est dans mon
expérience du monde que je perds tout !

¶

Si nous avons quelque peu voyagé, ce fut
dans le dessein
de n'être pas alourdi par notre léthargie.
Rien, cependant,
n'a entamé notre mépris d'être là.
Dans tous nos déplacements,
nous n'avons jamais découvert que du mauvais schiste.
En plus de notre ennui,
une lugubre indifférence nous répondait
de ville en ville.

¶

I close my eyes,
and the larches enter an ascetic phase.
I tremble,
and my body becomes pure fear
rather than the site of a shiver.
I grow smaller
down to the ivory of the ellipsis.
Infinity has had to draw near to me
for me to discover nothing. It is in my
experience of the world that I lose all!

¶

If we have travelled a little, it was
in the plan
of not being weighed down by our lethargy.
Nothing, however,
has shaken our scorn of being there.
In all our trips,
we only ever discovered bad shale.
Adding to our boredom,
a lugubrious indifference answered us
from town to town.

¶

En poésie
comme en tout autre domaine, ceux qui sont
sans honneur
réussissent dans leur entreprise.
A défaut d'accéder au sublime, les fourbes
se cantonnent dans l'illisible. Leur
complication langagière emprunte au monde
des scélérats.
La métaphore et l'inconduite partagent la même
racine.

¶

On lève les yeux
dans l'espoir de découvrir une image
conquérante,
et c'est un ciel flétri que l'on aperçoit.
Notre déconvenue
se poursuit d'altitude en altitude
et gagne bientôt
ce firmament desséché où meurt notre vision.
Comme les étoiles,
notre pensée expire dans une élévation sans issue.

¶

In poetry
as in every other domain, those
without honour
succeed in their initiative.
For want of acceding to the sublime, the swindlers
stick to the unreadable. Their
verbal complexities borrow from the world
of scoundrels.
Metaphor and misconduct share the same
root.

¶

We raise our eyes
in hope of discovering a conquering
image,
and we perceive a faded sky.
Our disappointment
continues from height to height
and soon reaches
those withered heavens where our vision dies.
Like the stars,
our great notions expire in a lofty dead end.

¶

Pendant un instant inépuisable, je me suis assis
près de la neige.
L'âme
qui me servait de refuge s'évanouit et devint
une immensité
appuyée sur l'immensité.
La perfection affluait et renonçait à tout recours
à la réflexion.
La neige
était à un doigt de renoncer à être neige.

¶

Les cerises sont serrées dans l'estomac
des noyaux.
Elles dorment
dans la constellation parfumée d'une petite amande
qui soupire
après le printemps.
Leur sommeil est sans vergogne.
Elles partagent le superbe détachement des fleurs
qui vont revenir et qui se croient
dispensées de la mort.

¶

For an inexhaustible instant, I sat down
by the snow.
My soul
which served as a refuge vanished and became
immensity
resting on immensity.
Perfection surged and abandoned all recourse
to reflection.
The snow
was within an inch of giving up as snow.

¶

The cherries are packed tight in the belly
of the stones.
They sleep
in the scented constellation of a small almond
which yearns for
spring.
Their sleep is shameless.
They share the superb detachment of flowers
which will return and believe themselves
excused from death.

¶

La nuit
vient avec l'instinct infaillible des cataclysmes.
Notre moi
est le signe avant-coureur d'une même perspective
de l'irréparable.
Nous pressentons depuis toujours que vivre
offusque l'espoir,
et qu'aucun plaisir ne rend le cœur prophétique.
Nous attendons
on ne sait quoi avec une ferveur insupportable.

¶

Le brouillard a élevé l'atmosphère à la hauteur
de la myopie.
Un foisonnement d'imprécisions transforme
le visible
en un pari sur l'esprit.
On hésite à faire le partage entre l'écume des
bouleaux
et les monuments inachevés de l'haleine.
Nous n'arrivons plus
à ignorer assez pour nos propres besoins.

¶

Night
falls with the infallible instinct of cataclysms.
Our self
is the foretoken of a same perspective
of the irreparable.
We have always sensed that living
offends hope,
and that no pleasure makes the heart a prophet.
With an unbearable fervour
we await we know not what.

¶

The fog has lifted the atmosphere to the height
of shortsightedness.
An abundance of imprecision transforms
the visible
into a wager on the mind.
We hesitate to divide the foam of
the birches
from the incomplete monuments of our breath.
We no longer manage
to be unknowing enough of our own needs.

¶

On soupçonne
que les ténèbres n'ont pas leur source
dans la nuit.
On devine
une opacité primitive, un
crépuscule
qui précède l'obscur.
On songe à une ombre très reculée qui devance
l'informe, et
qui montre que le noir
n'est que la couture d'une incohérence plus noire.

¶

Nul ne passe avec sa parole. Le corps respire
grâce
au poumon de l'imprononçable.
L'homme du verbe
n'est qu'un soupir entrelacé de nuit
L'air
suffoque lorsqu'on lui applique l'entrave
du signe.
A la fin,
chacun propose sa propre chair en guise de réponse.

¶

You suspect
that shadows do not stem from
the night.
You guess at
a primitive opacity, a
twilight
preceding the dark.
You think of shadows very far off which get ahead
of the formless, and
which show that blackness
is but the seam of a blacker incoherence.

¶

No one gets by with his speech. The body breathes
thanks
to the lung of the unpronounceable.
The man of words
is but a sigh intertwined with night.
The air
chokes when you fit it with the shackle
of the sign.
In the end,
each proposes his own flesh by way of reply.

¶

La neige est partout, et sa douceur désespère
les orateurs sacrés.
Il n'est plus un seul lieu où l'on puisse
placer une métaphore.
Son art
est si pur qu'il n'engendre pas la souffrance
d'une conviction.
L'ouïe est son verbe. C'est dans le clocher sans fin
de sa blancheur
que tintent mes plus beaux sous-entendus.

¶

Celui qui vit dans la simplicité entendra le roulement
du lointain.
L'angle
de ses pensées sera pulvérisé; ses
douleurs deviendront plus circonspectes.
Mais de grandes révolutions s'accompliront
en lui.
Ce sera surtout le cœur qui aura gagné:
sans se donner au monde,
il aura fait des bonds de géant dans sa propre nature.

¶

The snow is everywhere, and its softness drives
the sacred orators to despair.
There is no longer a single spot for you
to place a metaphor.
Its art
is so pure that it begets not the pain
of a conviction.
The hearing is its word. It is in the endless belfry
of its whiteness
that my finest understatements ring out.

¶

He who lives simply will hear the rumble
of distance.
The angle
of his thoughts will be smashed to bits; his
sorrows will grow more circumspect.
But great revolutions will be fulfilled
in him.
Above all it is the heart which will have triumphed:
without giving itself to the world,
it will have taken giant steps toward knowing itself.

¶

Figée dans sa crypte de glace, la fougère est
intacte,
mais écrasée par l'incorruption hivernale.
Son éternité
est retenue dans une écluse de marbre.
Elle atteint
le plus haut degré de sa concrétion dans une eau
devenue
un bloc de parcimonie.
Elle gît dans sa robuste dignité pétrifiée.

¶

Il est minuit.
Le charbon de l'heure se consume en braises
blanches.
Des ossements d'âmes tremblent
dans la grille.
Les ombres
se ruent sur les murs comme des rapaces
effilochés.
Nous demeurons seuls,
avec ce feu qui tente de réchauffer le feu.

¶

Frozen in its icy crypt, the fern is
intact,
but crushed by wintry non-decay.
Its eternity
is retained in a marble lock.
It attains
the highest degree of its concretion in a water
become
a bloc of parsimony.
It lies in its robust petrified dignity.

¶

It is midnight.
The coal of the hour burns out in white
embers.
Remains of souls flicker
in the grate.
The shadows
hurl themselves at the walls like torn
birds of prey.
We remain alone,
with that fire which tries to rekindle itself.

47

¶

Notre délabrement n'est pas une œuvre, ni
un oracle.
Notre moi
n'est pas une bourgade voisine
des Pléiades.
Nous ne présentons à personne l'hommage de notre
désastre. Et nous ne dédicaçons aucun de nos poèmes.
A l'âme,
il suffit de contempler le noir qui démontre
qu'il n'y a pas de noir.

¶

Je me réjouis de ce perpétuel
impossible
qui, en moi, fait apparaître tout projet comme
une souillure.
J'ai assez de superbe pour rester inactif pendant
mille ans.
C'est en vain que la nuit me pousse vers les lettres.
Quoique mon vers s'acharne,
ma poétique
n'est qu'un arrangement honoraire de mots.

¶

My ruin is not a work, nor
an oracle.
My self
is not a small town close to
the Pleiades.
I do not offer anyone the tribute of my
disaster. And I do not dedicate any of my poems.
For the soul,
it is enough to contemplate darkness which shows
darkness does not exist.

¶

I am delighted by this perpetual
impossible
which, in me, makes every project seem like
a taint.
I have enough fine arrogance to stay inactive for
a thousand years.
The night vainly pushes me toward literature.
Though my verse persists,
my poetics
is a merely honorary arrangement of words.

¶

Ce n'est pas la justesse
du propos
que l'on atteint lorsqu'une phrase est irréprochable,
c'est le sommeil.
La nuit est au sommet de l'expression.
Entre notre intuition et la lettre, il se forme
une brume, une sorte de requiem nébuleux
qui devient quelquefois un recueil de poésie.
Ce qu'on y dit
provoque l'obscurité de ce qui est tu.

¶

Quand l'âme
aurait récolté toutes les ivresses du néant,
elle resterait assoiffée d'abîmes
plus abrupts.
Elle poursuivrait une extinction plus
turbulente.
L'austérité de l'inexistant ne l'assouvit pas.
Aucun martyre ne la retient:
elle entend savourer
l'abus dont elle est l'allusion infernale.

¶

It is not the aptness
of the topic
which we achieve in an irreproachable phrase,
it is sleep.
Night is at the peak of expression.
Between our intuition and the word, a mist
forms, a kind of vague requiem
which sometimes becomes a volume of verse.
What we say therein
causes the abstruseness of what is silenced.

¶

When the soul
would have harvested all the ecstasy of nothingness,
it would remain thirsty for deeper
gulfs.
It would pursue a more turbulent
extinction.
The austerity of the inexistent fails to assuage it.
No martyr holds it back:
it intends to savour
the excess to which it hellishly alludes.

¶

La nuit est vieille et attend sous le porche,
tandis
que le blanc s'habille, jaillit et convertit
la lésine de l'ombre
en ducats rieurs.
Les flocons sont jeunes et se moquent
d'être sans feu ni lieu.
Pendant un instant,
leur candeur dépareillée
va faire de Noël une ville fortifiée.

¶

Tout à coup,
je me souvins de mes instruments de jardinage.
Le râteau,
qui attendait dans la grange pétrifiée,
et la faux
dont le tranchant s'était affiné par le froid.
Je ressentais la douleur poignante
de leur station.
Hors du pré, on eût dit qu'ils séjournaient comme moi,
au bord du vide.

¶

Night is old and waits beneath the porch, while
blank space dresses,
bursts forth and converts
the stinginess of shade
into cheerful ducats.
The flakes are young and scoff at
being without light or place.
For a moment,
their ill-matched candour
makes a fortress out of Christmas.

¶

All of a sudden,
I remembered my garden tools.
The rake,
which waited in the petrified barn,
and the scythe
whose cutting edge had been refined by the cold.
I felt the heartrending grief
of their position.
Away from the meadow, it seemed as if they were staying like
me, on the edge of the void.

¶

Il doit se trouver une médisance adroite
pour foudroyer
celui qui émet une pensée.
Il doit être une ironie qui perfore et met
un terme
au savoir enchevêtré des hommes. Ceux-ci brûlent
de toutes les ardeurs afin de prouver.
A défaut de bien voir, ils
cherchent obscurément la neige
dans la blancheur.

¶

Qui déchiffrera
l'énigme de la promenade que l'on fait lorsque
tout est effacé?
Par un raccourci connu de l'être,
on arrive
en un endroit ébouriffé de neiges sans avoir fait
de concessions
à l'équivoque du déplacement.
On se trouve là, dans
une essence qui n'est plus un affairement de lieux.

¶

There has to be a handy slander
to strike down
whoever ventures a thought.
There has to be an irony to puncture and put
a stop
to the muddled knowledge of men, who burn
with great passion so as to show proof.
Failing to see well, they
vaguely seek snow
in the whiteness.

¶

Who will make sense of
the enigmatic walk you take when
all is whitened out?
By a shortcut known to beings,
you arrive
in a place ruffled by snows, having conceded
nothing
to the doubt of the trip.
You find yourself there, in
an essence that is no longer a fuss of places.

¶

Le rôle
du regard est inconnu si ce n'est pour constater
que l'être
se maintient dans l'invisible
comme l'eau dévale la roche sans se tuer.
L'être
l'emporte sur l'épopée de l'œil.
L'objet
que l'on voit est le cauchemar d'un prisme,
une débâcle d'arpenteur.

¶

L'exercice des lettres n'est pas un comportement
distingué.
Le manque
de finesse et l'outrage à la bienséance
apparaissent dès le mot.
Celui qui expédie la neige à coups de syntaxe
indique
son manque de naissance.
Avec lui, la blancheur est réduite à la roture
du style.

¶

The role
of the gaze is unknown if it is not to observe
that being
remains in the invisible
as water rushes over the rock without killing itself.
Being
wins out over the epic of the eye.
The object
you see is a prismatic nightmare,
a surveyor's downfall.

¶

Literary practice is an undistinguished
performance.
The lack
of finesse and the affront to decorum
appear with the very first word.
You who dispatch the snow with syntactical blows
show
your lack of breeding.
With you, whiteness is reduced to a common
style.

¶

Belle
sans la disgrâce de la précaution, la neige
éblouissait
de toute son expérience précaire.
Sa légèreté
était un pressentiment qui précède
le toucher; on ignorait
si sa fourrure
frôlait la démence ou l'immatériel.
En la regardant, l'âme se savait regardée.

¶

Tête baissée dans leur mystère,
les oiseaux
ressemblaient à un colloque de bibelots taiseux.
Dans leurs ailes feutrées d'haleine,
ils respiraient
péniblement le granit de l'air.
Ils avaient
concentré leur immobilité dans quelques buissons,
là où la tranquillité se faisait fort d'être une âme.

¶

Beautiful
without the disgrace of precaution, the snow
dazzled
with all its fragile experience.
Its lightness
was a foreboding which precedes
touch; you did not know
if its fur
brushed madness or the immaterial.
Watching it, the soul knew it was being watched.

¶

Heads lowered in their mystery,
the birds
resembled a congress of silent trinkets.
In their wings matted by breath,
they inhaled
with difficulty the granite of the air.
They had
concentrated their stillness in a few bushes,
there where peace laid claim to be a soul.

¶

Nous comprîmes que la tempête de neige
était une réplique de nos déchirures.
Ce qui se pressait avec la horde
des flocons,
c'était la multitude des visages aimés qui
souffraient d'être effacés,
mais non apaisés.
Lorsque le calme revint, nous avons balayé notre cour
et avons rassemblé ces vagabonds de la mémoire
en un monceau de terrifiante indifférence.

¶

Il n'est rien de si fade que ce tourment désuet
des soirs d'hiver pendant lesquels,
faute d'amour,
on s'invente une âme.
On n'a pas le courage de lutter
contre cette volupté qui sent sa province.
Il se pourrait même
qu'on s'en réjouisse
comme s'il s'agissait du triomphe de
nos atermoiements.

¶

We understood that the snowstorm
was a replica of our jagged wounds.
What hurried on with the horde
of snowflakes,
was the multitude of beloved faces which
suffered being wiped out,
yet were not appeased.
When calm returned, we swept our yard
and gathered those vagabonds of memory
into a heap of frightful indifference.

¶

There is nothing as pointless as that outmoded torment
of winter evenings when,
for want of love,
we invent a soul for ourselves.
We do not have the courage to struggle
with that sensuality which smells of its province.
It is quite possible even
that we may delight in it
as if it meant the triumph of
our procrastinations.

¶

Que peut-on espérer
d'un infini
qui n'a aucune inclination pour le mot?
Que faut-il attendre d'une neige
qui n'établit
aucun rapport entre son signe et la pensée?
En quoi
peut-on convertir ce tout qui évite le tout?
Serait-ce une révélation
que d'ignorer ce que l'on doit à l'ignorance ?

¶

Elle ne se rendait en aucun lieu. Et c'est ainsi
que la neige
arriva comme un miracle.
Je reconnus son silence ajouré.
Son propos
tombait avec la tranquillité verticale
d'un proverbe
qui a longtemps hanté l'ouïe avant de connaître
la sagesse.
Elle avait le ton léger de la profondeur.

¶

What hope is there
for an infinity
which has no liking for the word?
What to expect of a snow
which establishes
no link between its sign and thought?
Into what
is to be converted that all which evades all?
Would it be a revelation
to know nothing of what we owe to ignorance?

¶

The snow was going nowhere. And so
it came
like a miracle.
I recognized its perforated silence.
Its utterance
fell with the vertical calm
of a proverb
which has long haunted the hearing before knowing
wisdom.
It had the light tone of depth.

¶

L'inclination à ne pas penser n'est pas un
versant nocturne.
C'est une pratique
par laquelle on rejette ce qui se présente sous
quelque dimension que ce soit.
Il n'est plus question d'être selon
un mode d'être.
On retrouve ainsi le temps qui n'est ni le temps,
ni l'effacement de celui-ci,
ni même une nuit d'hiver sous la neige.

¶

On commence un vers comme on dit bonsoir
à un passant.
On dépouille
furtivement celui-ci de son histoire.
On lui fait de silencieux reproches au sujet
du temps
qu'il a perdu à n'avoir pas été nous.
Puis on découvre que notre soliloque ne s'adresse
à personne.
C'est à ce moment que débute le destin du poème.

¶

The tendency not to think is not an
aspect of night.
It is a practice
by which you reject
what arises in whatever dimension.
It is no longer a question of being according to
any way of being.
Thus you regain time which is neither time,
nor its wiping out,
nor even a winter's night under the snow.

¶

We begin a verse like saying good evening
to a passer-by.
We strip him
furtively of his story.
We give him silent rebukes regarding
the time he has lost in not having been us.
Then we discover
that our monologue addresses
no one.
It is at this moment the poem's destiny begins.

¶

Lorsque la neige cessa de tomber, il neigeait
encore.
Un poudroiement minutieux
ajoutait
une frise posthume à l'œuvre de la blancheur.
Dans les zones indéfinies de la conscience,
on ressentait
la présence d'infimes froissements, comme une sorte
de mouvement abrasif du rien.
Tout tenait dans la plus petite fraction du possible.

¶

A force de ne rien nommer, l'incomparable
apparaît.
Il se lève
et plane au-dessus de nos flétrissures
verbales
comme un vent nocturne,
et berce
le sommeil étoile de ceux qui veillent.
Sans me toucher,
son faste me recouvre jusqu'aux épaules.

¶

When the snow stopped falling, it continued
to snow.
A minute powder
added
a border posthumous to the work of whiteness.
In the ill-defined zones of consciousness,
we felt
the presence of minute rustlings, like a kind of
abrasive movement of nothing.
All fitted the smallest fraction of the possible.

¶

By dint of naming nothing, the incomparable
appears.
It rises
and hovers above my verbal
stains
like a night wind,
and cradles
the starry sleep of those keeping watch.
Without touching me,
its splendour covers me up to the shoulders.

¶

Quelle leçon peut-on tirer de ce qui exige
que rien
ne soit vrai ?
Ce que l'on comprend
complique ce qui est déjà décousu.
Ce que l'esprit engendre
suscite une rancœur qui va jusqu'à l'érudition.
Même
ce que l'on ne conçoit pas est un lieu
mal fréquenté.

¶

La détresse rectiligne de la cité m'épuise.
Ses angles
contrarient le petit poème pastoral qui est en moi.
La ligne droite
est la plus longue traînée entre
deux gouffres, c'est
le traquenard du trajet.
La nuit venue,
c'est grâce à la courbe de la terre
que je m'endors.

¶

What lesson may we learn from that which demands
that nothing
be true?
What we understand
complicates what is already disjointed.
What the mind creates
gives rise to a rancour extending to scholarship.
Even
what we do not conceive of is a place
of ill repute.

¶

The rectilinear distress of the city tires me out.
Its angles
go against the little pastoral poem which is in me.
The straight line
is the longest trail between
two chasms, it is
the trap of the journey.
When night has fallen,
it is thanks to the curve of the earth
that I fall asleep.

69

¶

Celui qui eut une seule pensée claire
peut déclarer combien sa vie fut étrange.
Cette unique lumière fera de lui
un de ces êtres intermédiaires qui s'éveillent
lorsqu'on descend la pente
du sommeil. Il sera tenu pour quelqu'un qui
n'aspire à aucun triomphe et ne consent
à posséder aucun bien.
Il sera perclus de transparence,
et personne ne voudra vivre avec lui.

¶

Parfois, dans la nuit,
un oiseau chante et ne se fait pas entendre.
A cet instant,
la pensée obéit, c'est-à-dire, elle
s'abstient. Puis elle redevient pensée. Elle
réintègre la distraction de l'entendement
et de l'écoute. Elle
nous abandonne dans l'oubli du temps
où l'on se trouvait
dans ce chant d'oiseau que l'oiseau ne chantait pas.

¶

He who had a single clear thought
may assert how strange was his life.
That sole light will make of him
one of those indeterminate beings who awaken
when you descend the slope
of sleep. He will be taken for someone who
does not aspire to any triumph or consent
to own any worldly goods.
He will be paralyzed by clarity,
and no one will wish to live with him.

¶

Sometimes, in the night,
a bird sings without making itself heard.
At that moment,
thought obeys, that is to say, it
abstains. Then it becomes thought once more. It
reinstates the distraction of understanding
and of listening. It
abandons us to the oblivion of time
where we found ourselves
in that bird song unsung by the bird.

¶

La fontaine
était tenue dans l'étau des glaces. Son
jaillissement
avait fait un douloureux retour à l'opaque.
Toute certitude à propos de l'eau
était suspendue. Il y avait de quoi applaudir
à ce retrait de limpidité: il augmentait la
contemplation d'une perplexité plus grande, il
ajoutait
la rigidité à ce qui était déjà peu crédible.

¶

Sous la neige, le potager est invérifiable.
On ne distingue plus
les légumes que par le souvenir.
On s'en tient
à une conception immaculée des primeurs.
La laitue est captive
d'un invincible confit de givre,
et la fraise n'est plus qu'un état d'âme.
A nous,
les plaisirs de la gastronomie transcendantale!

¶

The fountain
was held in the vice grip of the frosts. Its
gushing
had made a sorrowful return to the opaque.
All certainty regarding water
was on hold. There was something to applaud
in this retreat of clarity: it increased the
contemplation of a greater confusion, it
added
stiffness to what was already barely credible.

¶

Beneath the snow, the kitchen garden cannot be confirmed.
We discern
the vegetables from memory alone.
We confine ourselves
to an immaculate conception of the early crop.
The lettuce is captive
to an invincible pickle of frost,
and the strawberry is no more than a state of mind.
To us,
the pleasures of transcendental gastronomy!

¶

Là où tombe la neige se tient depuis l'éternité
la neige inqualifiable,
celle
de l'impénétrable énigme qui n'est point.
Je m'emploie
à réduire l'écart entre la blancheur et la blancheur.
En vain! La neige est tombée
en même temps que la neige, et mon identité
en fut décolorée.
Je n'ai que le verbe pour me déclarer démuni.

¶

L'être se détache de la nuit et entraîne des débris
d'univers
qui deviennent l'univers.
L'être se précipite sur moi, et
je deviens à mon tour bâtisseur de précipices. Car
l'insigne du néant est sur lui
comme l'arrogance est sur moi.
Il est tyrannique
et fragile:
c'est pourquoi l'âme le reçoit comme un prince brimé.

¶

Where the snow falls, the unspeakable snow
holds on forever,
that snow
of the impenetrable enigma which is not.
I devote myself
to narrowing the gap between whitenesses.
In vain! The snow has fallen
at the same time as the snow, and my identity
was faded by it.
I have but words to speak my powerlessness.

¶

Being detaches itself from the night and drags debris
of universe
which become the universe.
Being rushes in on me, and
I become in turn builder of brinks. For
the emblem of nothingness is on it
as arrogance is on me.
It is tyrannical
and fragile:
it is why the soul receives it like an initiated prince.

¶

Les petits tableaux de l'enfance reviennent
à la mémoire.
La chaleur ambiguë des soirées
en famille,
et les minuscules incidents parmi les flocons
transforment
leur douceur en de puérils
arcanes. On ne fait plus le partage
entre les allusions
à la mort et le bonheur d'avoir été innocent.

¶

Touché
par un demi-jour intérieur, l'observateur,
quelquefois, devient attentif, et
se garde d'observer.
De cette vision exemplaire, il
ne retient qu'un tronc élagué des branches
du visible.
Ne voyant rien,
il embrasse le paysage sans feuilles et sans
défaut. Il contemple le site intouché de l'être.

¶

The small scenes of childhood return
to memory.
The ambiguous warmth of family
evenings,
and the tiny incidents among the snowflakes
transform
their softness into childish
mysteries. You no longer divide
the allusions
to death from the joy of having been innocent.

¶

Moved
by an interior half-light, the observer,
sometimes, becomes attentive and
wary of observing.
Of this exemplary vision, he
retains but a pruned limb of the branches
of the visible.
Seeing nothing,
he embraces the flawless, leafless landscape.
He gazes upon the unmoved site of being.

¶

L'immense est scellé.
Un nœud de neige étrangle celui qui emprunte
l'étendue.
L'impalpable ici de la blancheur est une entorse
au lieu.
L'âme
se trouve enfin assez de minceur pour s'accorder
au lointain
sans s'y rendre; elle accepte
l'incertitude qui participe au savoir du Nord.

¶

Le mât du néant est visible
à partir de n'importe quel émerveillement.
Il se dresse
au milieu de l'écume colossale qui sans cesse
régénère la même absence.
C'est une perfection poussée par un infini
contraire.
Sa ligne
est le tombeau vertical qui enferme le tout
dans le tout.

¶

The boundless is sealed.
A knot of snow strangles whoever enters
the area.
Here the intangible of the whiteness twists
the place.
The soul
finally finds itself slim enough to blend
with the distance
without going there; it accepts
the uncertainty which shares in the knowledge of the North.

¶

The mast of nothingness is in sight
from the point of no matter what wonderment.
It sticks up
amid the colossal foam which endlessly
restores the same absence.
It is a perfection driven by a contrary
infinity.
Its outline
is the vertical tomb which encloses all
within all.

¶

Je ne tolère plus d'avoir la respiration coupée
par le verbe.
Les phrases rétrécies qui se veulent
des strophes
tiennent mon souffle à l'écart.
Hélas,
ma façon d'aspirer n'est plus un élan!
Combien de paroles faudra-t-il réprimer
avant d'éprouver
ce qui n'est pas conçu sans me compromettre?

¶

D'aucuns utilisent le traîneau. D'autres,
leurs facultés intellectuelles.
Dans les deux cas,
on passe légèrement sur les choses.
On dérange
quelques finesses au passage.
Puis,
réticente à toute trace durable, la neige se ravise.
Tout n'aura été
qu'une problématique de la surface.

¶

I no longer stand having my breath cut
by words.
The shrunken phrases which claim
to be stanzas
take my breath away.
Alas,
my way of aspiring is no longer a rush!
How many words must be stifled
before feeling
what I cannot think without self-compromise?

¶

Some use the sled. Others,
their powers of mind.
In both cases,
you skim over things.
You disturb
a few niceties in the process.
Then,
disinclined to any lasting trace, the snow has second thoughts.
All will only have been
a surface problematic.

¶

Vous souffrez un peu, c'est-à-dire, vous tenez
dans les limites
propres aux hommes d'intelligence moyenne.
Vous nourrissez des sentiments ambigus
à l'égard de l'infini.
Votre coeur a gardé la nuance inquiète
de l'enfant
porteur d'un oiseau en cage.
Vous entendez parler dans la nuit: c'est votre
respiration que vous prenez pour un commentaire.

¶

Celui qui écoute attentivement en soi,
n'entend rien.
Il n'est plus traversé par la matière métaphorique
de l'ouïe:
il a l'oreille collée à l'impossible.
S'il pense fortement,
il n'est plus nulle part et passe ainsi sa première
nuit à la belle étoile. Il n'est plus astreint
à désigner ce qu'il éprouve. Il comprend
que son vide le rapproche de tout.

¶

You suffer a little, that is to say, you stay
within the bounds
proper to men of average mind.
You nurture ambiguous feelings
about infinity.
Your heart has kept the anxious nuance
of the child
carrying a bird in a cage.
You hear talking in the night: it is your
breathing which you take for a remark.

¶

He who listens closely in itself,
hears nothing.
He is no longer pierced by the metaphorical matter
of the heard:
he has an ear glued to the impossible.
If he thinks powerfully,
he is no longer anywhere and thus spends his first
night out in the open. He is no longer compelled
to name what he experiences. He understands
that his void brings him closer to all.

¶

Le rien m'étouffe aussi.
Il y a quelque chose d'impardonnable
dans
ce qui est conçu, dans ce qui dure.
Et l'infini suinte le tourment.
O que la nuit est longue
à obtenir la fin de la nuit de quelqu'un!
Serait-ce une grâce trop âprement convoitée
que ce parfait
et imprenable non-lieu du moi?

¶

Nous attendons
que la signification soit retirée de la neige.
Sa blancheur
l'emporte sur les astuces de la rhétorique.
Elle est instaurée
avant notre dictée et fait étinceler
le givre sans avoir recours
à l'hypothétique bonheur de l'expression.
La plaine enneigée
n'est-elle pas aussi problématique qu'un mot juste?

¶

Nothing stifles me too.
There is something inexcusable
in
what is thought up, in what lasts.
And infinity oozes torment.
O how the night is long
in granting the end of someone's night!
Would it be a pardon too bitterly craved:
that perfect,
unassailable non-suit of the self?

¶

We await
meaning to be drawn from the snow.
Its whiteness
triumphs over rhetorical tricks.
It is set up
before our use of words and makes ice
sparkle without recourse
to the dubious felicity of expression.
Is not the snowy plain
as tricky as a well-turned phrase?

¶

Je traverse l'émail des prés. Mes pas brisent
le tapis de silice,
et envoient d'innombrables toupies de lumières noires
et irisées
au loin,
jusqu'à l'éparpillement de mes pupilles.
Les éclats
du gel criblent mon passage.
Je ne suis
qu'une frise d'haleine autour d'un regard.

¶

Ce n'est pas mourir
que de faire ses adieux à l'intendance.
On devient naturellement
lointain
sans que cela soit le propre d'une vie révolue.
Sous les couches successives
de l'oubli
notre temps gagne en épaisseur.
Ce qui n'est plus le moi
puise à pleines mains dans l'abondance de l'être.

¶

I cross the enamel of the fields. My footsteps break
the vitreous carpet,
and send endless spinning-tops of black and iridescent
lights
into the distance,
as far as the scattering of my pupils.
The scintillating
frost sifts my crossing.
I am but
a frieze of breath around a look.

¶

It is not dying,
only bidding adieu to supplies.
We naturally become
distant
without that being the mark of a bygone life.
Beneath the successive layers
of forgetting
our time gains in depth.
What is no longer the self
draws fully on the richness of being.

¶

Il est des hommes qui exhalent une odeur
d'antérieur.
Ils se répandent dans l'air
comme des effluves d'excavations fangeuses. Ils
sont comme ces émanations
que l'on respire lorsqu'on déterre la terre.
Leurs pensées
sont fétides comme les relents de l'Histoire.
Ils n'accordent
leur confiance qu'à ce qui relève de la mort.

¶

On ouvre le livre de la neige,
et l'on tombe sur ce passage où un insecte
a gravé sa mort
dans la blancheur du papier.
Il gît
dans le récit comme un monogramme raidi
par le froid.
Et la brindille de son corps
plonge ma lecture de l'hiver dans une sorte
de post-scriptum funéraire.

¶

There are men who give off a smell
of beforehand.
They spread through the air
like miasmas of muddy excavations. They
resemble those fumes
you inhale when you dig up the earth.
Their thoughts
are fetid like the stench of history.
They put their trust
only in what matters for death.

¶

I open the book of the snow,
and I happen upon that piece where an insect
has carved its death
in the whiteness of the paper.
It lies
in the story like a monogram stiffened
by cold.
And its twiglike body
sinks my winter reading into a kind
of funereal postscript.

¶

L'être
inspire ce qui le dissout. Il est la noire
extase
qui éveille le don d'aphasie prophétique.
Un mot
le rend impénétrable.
Un dessein
fait de lui l'étincelle propre à allumer le feu
des nations. Son commencement
frappe l'univers d'apoplexie originelle.

¶

Ce à quoi tout est donné sans coup férir
ne se dégrade pas
dans le devenir.
Ce qui est atteint
ne le fut pas à la manière dont on rend l'incendie
solaire
comptable de la violette.
Afin d'éviter le pire, il faut se considérer nul.
Pour être monde, le monde
s'est déployé hors de l'inclémence de l'Histoire.

¶

Being
inspires what dissolves it. It is the dark
ecstasy
which awakens the gift of prophetic aphasia.
One word
makes it impenetrable.
One intention
makes of it the spark used to light the fire
of nations. Its beginning
strikes the universe with original apoplexy.

¶

That to which all is given without any problem
does not debase itself
in the future.
What is attained
was not done so in the way you hold the solar
fire
answerable to the violet.
So as to avoid the worst, you must deem yourself nothing.
To be world, the world
has stretched itself beyond the pitilessness of history.

¶

La nuit abuse de notre difficulté de voir.
Elle nous menace de
ce qu'on ne voit pas et rend ainsi les choses
plus absurdes qu'invisibles.
Elle s'approprie le compliment de constellation
noire.
Sous ses auspices,
on se préparait à l'apaisement d'un soir
anodin, et c'est dans l'arrogance d'un mystère
que l'on tombe.

¶

La nostalgie est insatiable. Elle se sent
étriquée
dans la fatalité même.
Elle réclame
les plus grands effondrements de l'univers pour
éblouir le noir qui est en elle.
Son anxiété prend naissance dans la propension
qu'a l'être à n'être pas. Elle jalouse ce rien
qui reste dans le nid après le départ des oisillons.
Elle attend d'être dévorée par sa propre nature.

¶

Night exploits our difficulty in seeing.
It threatens us with
what we do not see and so makes things
more absurd than invisible.
It adapts itself to the compliment of black
galaxy.
Under its auspices,
we prepared ourselves for the calmness of a meaningless
evening, and found ourselves falling
into an arrogant mystery.

¶

Nostalgia is insatiable. It feels
mean spirited
even in misfortune.
It demands
the greatest crumblings of the universe so as
to bedazzle the darkness within it.
Its anxiety is born of the tendency
of being not to be. It is jealous of that nothing
which stays in the nest after the fledglings have flown.
It waits to be consumed by its own nature.

¶

Seuls les séraphins obtus
regardent la lumière comme une séparation
de l'ombre.
Ils ne voient pas
la charnière d'air noir qui commande la porte
du soleil.
Quand il y aurait une aube, elle serait ajustée
à la taille de la nuit.
Quand il y aurait un instant de grâce, il serait
pris dans l'épaisseur du désastre.

¶

La seule chose qui est n'est pas.
Aussi, ce n'est pas se méprendre que de ne rien
admettre.
Voyez l'âme, elle s'accommode de son tombeau!
Ce que nous énonçons
clairement est un cloaque tapageur, une barque
ancrée dans le mutisme.
Ce n'est pas dans l'étoffe d'une preuve
que les météores taillent leur vitesse embrasée,
mais dans le noir qui les précède et les suit.

¶

Only the dimwitted seraphim
regard light as a separation
from shade.
They do not see
the hinge of black air which controls the gate
of the sun.
When dawn would come, it would be adjusted
to the size of the night.
When a moment of grace would arise, it would be
caught up in the depth of the disaster.

¶

The only thing that is, is not.
So, it is not self-contempt to admit
nothing.
See the soul, it endures its tomb!
What we express
clearly is a showy cesspool, a small boat
anchored in silence.
It is not in the fabric of a proof
that meteors cut their blazing speed
but in the blackness which precedes and follows them.

¶

Nous ne pouvons continuer de supplier qu'on
nous accorde
des déserts plus arides, qu'on nous
fasse connaître des mythes et des hivers
plus intacts.
C'est pourquoi
nous voulons réduire notre absolu en de courtes
phrases que l'on peut répéter sans recourir
à l'esprit. Nous voulons réprimer
tout soupir qui ne coïncide pas avec l'air.

¶

Ne parlons plus de l'infini
comme d'un concile de toutes les distances.
Cet interminable lieu
que l'étendue déploie est l'étendard transparent
d'une plaie.
Pourquoi écouter ce clairon absolu
qui annonce
que le déboire est répandu dans l'espace?
Comme notre respiration,
le dehors est fermé de l'intérieur.

¶

We cannot carry on begging
to be granted
more arid deserts, to be
made acquainted with more unblemished
myths and winters.
It is why
we want to reduce our absolute to short
phrases that may be repeated without recourse
to the mind. We want to repress
every sigh which does not coincide with air.

¶

Let us talk no more of the infinite
as of a council of every distance.
That interminable place
which a stretch unfurls is the transparent standard
of a wound.
Why listen to that peremptory bugle
which announces
that setbacks are widespread in space?
Like our breathing,
the outside is closed off from the inside.

¶

Dans le cliquetis des flocons,
on entend
une rumeur que l'on pourrait comparer au
discours de la conscience.
Ces bruits
nous font franchir la barrière des glossaires.
Notre âme
se refait continuellement ainsi, au détour
de l'équivoque, lorsque
les choses ne nous disent rien de cohérent.

¶

Une bise féroce harcelait les flocons novices.
– N'entre pas dans les vues
du verbe, me fit le vent persifleur,
le silence se taît mieux; il n'est de
réel
que dans ce qui est indicible.
Je me préparais ainsi à une parfaite mortification
dans les aspérités du froid, lorsque
ce poème vint,
tel une intrigue patiemment ourdie.

¶

In the clinking of snowflakes,
we hear
a sound which we might compare to
the speech of conscience. These noises
make us smash
the barrier of vocabularies.
In this way
our soul reconstitutes itself constantly, following
the equivocal, when
things tell us nothing coherent.

¶

A ferocious blast was pestering the inexperienced snowflakes.
– Do not enter the sights
of the word, the mocking wind told me,
silence quietens itself best; the
real
lies only in what is unsayable.
So I was readying myself to be perfectly mortified
in the harshness of cold, when
this poem came along,
like a patiently hatched plot.

¶

Nous avons dépassé ce qui signifie. Nous voici
aux avant-postes
d'une révélation dépourvue
de substance.
Pour éviter
ce qui serait une affectation de plus, nous
avons renoncé
à l'éclat du dilemme.
Nous nous sommes mis à désirer davantage
qu'une conclusion.

¶

La contradiction entre la neige et la neige
atteint
son apogée dans ce qui sépare l'être
de l'être.
C'est en s'inspirant de la pénurie
d'affirmations
que toute chose évite de donner dans le faux.
Ce que le poète commente
est essentiellement
la négation qui le révèle à soi-même.

¶

We have gone beyond meaning. Here we are
at the outposts
of a revelation devoid
of substance.
In order to avoid
what would be one more affectation, we have abandoned
the glitter
of the dilemma.
We have begun to desire more
than a conclusion.

¶

The contradiction between snow and snow
reaches
its peak in what separates being
from being.
It is by gaining inspiration from the paucity
of affirmations
that everything avoids lapsing into the false.
What the poet explains
is mainly
the negation which reveals him to himself.

¶

On ne voit rien, sauf
cette blancheur qui confine au coup de ciseau
dans l'œil.
Maintenant,
le regard se nourrit de sa propre pulpe.
Nous ne frôlons plus
que le bord le plus proche de nous-mêmes.
On s'adapte
progressivement à ce qu'on ne vérifie point.
On ne se sent plus exposé au moi ni au monde.

¶

Une première chute de neige permit une
subite
simplification de l'étendue.
On ne sépara plus
les hameaux et les clochers qui se succédaient
à l'horizon.
Les enfants comprirent spontanément et lancèrent
leur traîneau
sur l'unique flocon qui recouvrait tous
les coteaux.

¶

We see nothing except
that whiteness verging on a scissor stab
in the eye.
Now,
the gaze feeds on its own pulp.
We no longer skirt anything
but the edge closest to ourselves.
We adapt
gradually to what we cannot confirm.
We no longer feel exposed to the self or to the world.

¶

A first snowfall allowed a
sudden
simplification of the area.
You no longer made out
the hamlets and church towers which followed one another
to the horizon.
The children understood at once and launched
their sled
on the only snowflake
which covered all the slopes.

¶

Vient l'époque
où l'on se soumet à l'intraduisible.
Le refus de la pensée
atteint alors son plus prestigieux avènement.
Toute chose
qui tente de s'accroître par la vérité est
repoussée.
Ce qui n'est pas assujetti au néant est chassé
de l'esprit.
On abandonne la poésie au milieu de ses imprécations.

¶

Il ne reste plus rien dont on veuille se faire
une opinion.
On ne demande plus aux choses de pâlir
devant une définition.
Nous ne donnons plus à l'univers son contrepoids
de réponses.
Sans faire de bruit,
la nuit et l'entendement échangent leur cécité.
On se sent
enfin aussi parfaitement cohérent que le néant.

¶

There comes an age
when you yield to the untranslatable.
Refusing to think
then has its most prestigious accession.
Everything
which tries to grow from truth is
rebuffed.
What is not yoked to nothingness is chased
from the mind.
You abandon poetry amid its curses.

¶

There is nothing left on which we wish to have
an opinion.
We no longer ask things to pale
in the face of a definition.
We no longer give the universe its counterweight
of answers.
Without making any noise,
night and understanding swap their blindness.
At last
we feel as perfectly coherent as nothingness.

¶

La neige s'approchait des dormeurs et rehaussait
leur immobilité
d'ornements indescriptibles.
Elle descendait sur leur sommeil
comme
une première version de l'infini.
Elle posait son étoffe doucement
sur leur corps,
et tentait de leur faire rendre l'âme
sans les déranger.

¶

Le repos des sapins est une apoplexie
friable,
un labyrinthe d'aspérités fragiles. La neige
couvre ce prodige
avec la prudence d'un verbe qui essaie de dire
au lieu de nuire.
Le tremblement
de l'haleine suffirait pour détruire ce coma.
Notre silence
est une préparation à cette quiétude d'aiguilles.

¶

The snow came close to the sleepers and enhanced
their stillness
with indescribable embellishments.
It dropped into their sleep
like
a first version of infinity.
It laid its fabric softly
on their bodies,
and tried to make them yield their souls
without disturbing them.

¶

The repose of firs is a powdery
apoplexy,
a labyrinth of fragile harshness. The snow
covers this prodigy
with the prudence of a word trying to tell
instead of doing harm.
The quivering
of breath would suffice to destroy this coma.
Our silence
prepares us for this quietude of needles.

¶

Lorsque je ne vis plus rien,
je fis
cette déduction que la plaine était plus avancée
que mes métaphores.
Je m'arrêtai pour considérer
cette absence
dont je venais de toucher le corps indémontrable.
Toute la neige m'était présentée; je
ne pouvais recueillir d'autre indication d'elle
que son étincelant éloignement.

¶

Il est perspicace celui qui n'entend rien et qui
construit sa demeure
dans l'inaudible. Il s'entasse dans
ce qui se retire.
II se quitte
et devient la clef de voûte d'une ouïe sans appui.
Il échoue
avec intensité
dans les bruits indigènes de la blancheur. Il
écoute son propre discours infondé.

¶

When I no longer saw anything,
I made
this deduction that the plain extended
beyond my metaphors.
I stopped to mull over
this absence
whose unprovable body I had just touched.
The entire snow was offered to me; I
could not get any other sign of it
than its sparkling distance.

¶

Perceptive is he who hears nothing and who
builds his home
in the inaudible. He crams himself into
what recedes.
He leaves himself
and becomes the linchpin of an unsupported ear.
He is beached
intensely
in the native noise of whiteness. He
listens to his own groundless speech.

¶

Les ailes basses de la forêt ont touché
notre mémoire.
On retrouve l'obscurité exaspérée de l'enfance.
La nuit
suggère que tout climat familial est celui
de la terreur.
Il est une brutalité absolue
dont l'état le plus pur est la parenté.
Cela commence
à la naissance, comme une incision dans notre verbe.

¶

Dans la vocifération blanche
d'une tempête,
on distingue quelquefois un flocon méritant.
Mais le tumulte ne peut se
l'adjoindre.
Délaissé,
il tombera seul, dans la lourdeur tragique
du temps.
Hormis le poème,
il n'est rien qui puisse aller à sa rencontre.

¶

The forest's low wings have touched
our memory.
We rediscover the exasperated darkness of childhood.
Night
suggests that every family atmosphere is one
of terror.
There is an absolute brutality
whose purest state is kith and kin.
It begins
at birth, like a cut in our speech.

¶

In the white clamour
of a storm,
you sometimes make out a worthy snowflake.
But the tumult cannot
take it on.
Forsaken,
it falls alone, in the tragic weight
of time.
Save for the poem,
nothing can go forth to meet it.

¶

Toute chose démontrée
provoque l'insurrection de l'impossible.
O imprudente clarté!
Nous voulons nous enfouir avec les oiseaux qui,
la nuit venue,
refusent la définition de la forêt, mais
s'en vont dormir en elle.
Comme celui qui dessine sait que le trait
le détériore,
nous ne voulons pas vivre de ce que nous comprenons.

¶

Puisque le silence allie la précaution
à la tristesse,
puisque
ce que l'on pense ne doit pas être pensé,
pourquoi s'adonner encore
à l'art des mots?
Si la neige avait attendu
la parole,
il lui aurait fallu une éternité de plus
pour amener la blancheur au flocon.

¶

Everything proven
causes the impossible to revolt.
O foolish clarity!
We want to fly off with the birds who,
at night,
reject the forest's definition, yet
go there to sleep.
As he who draws knows that the line
harms him,
we do not want to live on what we understand.

¶

Since silence unites precaution
with sadness,
since
what you think ought not to be thought,
why still give yourself up
to the art of the word?
If the snow
had awaited
speech, it would have needed another eternity
to bring whiteness to the flake.

¶

Le soir descend vers quatre heures. Nous sommes
las du jour
comme d'un apprentissage qui ne s'achève pas.
Nous nous écroulons
comme la réputation des livres.
Le peu de clarté qu'il y eut
s'attarde
sur le visage des hommes qui attendent l'héritage
qui ne viendra pas.
On hésite à saluer ceux qui regardent notre visage.

¶

Je ne puis plus dissimuler
qu'il n'y eut jamais de véritable dessein
en moi.
Ne rien prétendre, comme je le fis autrefois,
était un plan concerté.
Cultiver
la douceur de l'irrésolution, me fonder
sur l'hésitation des mots pour gagner un peu
d'être … tout cela était feint!
La nuit a trahi mon manque d'intention.

¶

Evening draws in around four. We are
tired of the day
as of an unfinished apprenticeship.
We collapse
like the reputation of books.
What little daylight there was
lingers
on the face of men who await the legacy
which will not come.
We hesitate to greet those who look at our face.

¶

I can no longer pretend
that sometimes I have had true designs
within me.
To claim nothing, as I did before,
was a concerted plan.
To cultivate
the gently irresolute, to base myself
on the hesitation of words in order to gain a little
being ... all that was feigned!
Night has betrayed my lack of intention.

¶

L'impossible est l'inépuisable somme du poème.
Il est le rien inabordable
qui brûle d'un feu
rentré
et qui allume la mystérieuse incapacité
de dire.
Il déploie l'insurmontable et ouvre la béance
de ce qui est surmonté.
Il ressemelle sans cesse la même pensée
qui ne se prête au pied d'aucun voyageur.

¶

Fort
de ce que la neige proclame que son essence
est un incessant éloignement
de la blancheur,
le verbe
aspire à n'être plus exprimable.
Tout se tient dans l'axe de son être propre
et le dit en s'abstenant de le dire. C'est ainsi
que je perds un bras
chaque fois que j'écris le mot neige.

¶

The impossible is the unlimited sum of the poem.
It is the inaccessible nothing
which burns with a suppressed
fire
and which lights up the strange inability
to speak.
It shows off the insuperable and opens wide
what is overcome.
Endlessly it resoles the same thought
which lends itself to no traveller's foot.

¶

With the snow
proclaiming that its essence
is a ceaseless distancing
from whiteness,
the word
aspires to be no longer expressible.
Everything clings to the axis of its own being
and speaks it while abstaining from doing so. It is thus
that I lose an arm
each time I write the word snow.

¶

Nous conjuguons comme des diables, et prétendons
construire un temps nouveau
à l'aide du temps de la fable.
Nous entendons nous soustraire à l'éphémère
en nous associant
à une parole qui n'est qu'une exposition
d'un temps défunt.
A la fin,
on se demande sous le couvert de quel imparfait
on peut dire qu'il fait nuit.

¶

Ce qui commence est consacré à la nuit. Aucun
abîme n'est fait autrement
que de son arrivée.
Il n'est pas jusqu'au néant qui, en se privant d'état,
n'ouvre une brèche.
On soupçonne que ce qui vient
vise
à supplanter le désœuvrement foncier.
Le ciel est dit noir
lorsque nous y voyons une imitation du devenir.

¶

We conjugate like fiends, and claim
to make up a new time
with the help of the tense of the tale.
We agree to shield ourselves from the ephemeral
by joining forces
with a word which merely exhibits
a bygone time.
In the end,
we wonder under cover of what imperfect
we may say it is night.

¶

What begins is devoted to the night. No
gulf is made other
than from its arrival.
By lack of being, everything (and nothing)
opens up a gap.
We suspect that what comes
aims
to displace the basic idleness.
The sky is said to be dark
when we see in it an imitation of the future.

¶

Il n'y avait aucun repère pour mesurer
le degré
d'égarement des voyageurs.
L'hérésie de la destination et du trompe-l'œil
régnait partout.
On suivait un chemin
qui n'aboutissait ni dans la plaine ni dans un soliloque.
La neige
consacrait l'intarissable horreur de tout lieu.

¶

Il est éloquent et redoutable, le refus de l'être.
Sa réticence
à exécuter la menace du réel
fait que tout spécule et échoue sur le verbe.
Chacune de ses réparties est un port
gelé
où tout débarque au milieu de l'immobile.
Je m'étonne
d'exister selon son abstention fondatrice.
Sa nuit sied aux âmes qui ne conviennent de rien.

¶

There was no landmark to measure
how far afield
the travellers had strayed.
The heresy of destination and of *trompe-l'oeil*
held sway everywhere.
You followed a path
ending neither on the plain nor in a monologue.
The snow
sanctified the unfailing horror of every place.

¶

It is eloquent and fearsome, the refusal of being.
Its reticence
in carrying out the threat of the real
causes all to bank on and wash up in the word.
Each of its retorts is a frozen
port
where all disembarks amid stillness.
I am amazed
to exist according to its founding abstention.
Its night suits souls who agree on nothing.

¶

L'être incline ses miroirs vers celui qui ne
s'y reconnaît pas.
Son soleil
laisse intacte la pupille qui renonce
au poids de l'œil.
Il éclaire
son propre dilemme sans jeter la lumière hors
de ses gonds.
Pour la première fois,
la transparence n'est pas une contrefaçon.

¶

Il n'y a ni forêt ni contemplation
de la forêt,
mais une distance intérieure aggravée
de branches.
Depuis que l'espace a épousé
le vocabulaire,
je tiens le feuillage en suspicion.
Dans la plus idyllique des clairières, je me garde
de cette absence d'arbres
qui contrefait je ne sais quoi de sylvain.

¶

Being tilts its mirrors toward he who fails
to recognize himself in them.
Its sun
leaves intact the pupil which abandons
the weight of the eye.
It lights up
its own dilemma without casting any light outside
its hinges.
For the first time,
transparency is not counterfeit.

¶

There is neither forest nor thought
of the forest,
but an inner distance worsened
by branches.
Since space has wed
vocabulary,
I hold the foliage suspect.
In the most idyllic of clearings, I am wary
of this absence of trees
which mimics something sylvan.

¶

La lune a révélé
la ruine mitoyenne qui se dresse entre la mélancolie
et la blancheur.
Elle a dévoilé
la pâleur qu'affectionnent les solitaires,
ceux pour qui la tristesse
est un diamant de suif.
A la faveur de sa clarté inaccomplie,
on hésite
à distinguer un spectre d'un badigeon d'âme.

¶

Après qu'il eut neigé
et que le petit bois où je m'engage d'ordinaire
fut recouvert,
il restait un débris de sentier qui s'évanouissait
dans le taillis.
Les réserves minérales
de la sérénité
étaient intactes. La blancheur y était vierge
de tout scepticisme. Il me suffisait
d'être naturel, c'est-à-dire sans envergure.

¶

The moon has revealed
the common ruin rising up between melancholy
and whiteness.
It has unveiled
the pallor which loners are fond of,
those for whom sadness
is a candle-grease diamond.
Aided by its unaccomplished brightness,
they hesitate
to discern a ghost from a whitewashed soul.

¶

After it had snowed
and the small wood where I normally go
was covered over,
a fragment of footpath remained only then to vanish
into the thicket.
The mineral reserves
of serenity
remained intact. The whiteness there was devoid
of all scepticism. It was enough for me
to be natural, that is to say, without scope.

¶

Il y eut quelques instants de sublime
aveuglement,
puis la bourrasque cessa, et la nuit dut s'avouer
vaincue.
Ça et là,
on reconnaissait les traces d'une destinée
qui avait été colossale,
et qui se présentait maintenant
sous les dehors d'une simple soirée d'hiver.

¶

Je me fais rare et taciturne afin que mon
parler
ne soit pas pris pour une hypocrisie couronnée
de givre.
Mon écrit
est une hallucination remise à neuf
à l'occasion des grands froids.
Si je m'exprime, je fends l'indescriptible
en mille. Aussi, j'accepte
que la neige se charge de mes propres subtilités.

¶

There were several moments of sublime
blindness,
then the squall stopped, and night had to admit itself
beaten.
Here and there,
you recognized the tracks of a destiny
once colossal,
and which now appeared
beneath the cloak of a plain winter's evening.

¶

I make myself scarce and silent so that my
speech
be not taken for hypocrisy crowned
by frost.
My written word
is a hallucination done up like new
on the occasion of great cold spells.
If I express myself, I split the indescribable
into a thousand parts. Also, I accept
that the snow takes care of my own subtleties.

¶

Le bruit
que fait la neige rend à peine perceptible
le fragment d'être
qui tombe et se pense en tant que fragment
de neige.
Il faudrait une ouïe infléchie et douce
pour convertir
cette légèreté-là en une pratique du monde.
Une fois de plus, mon propos, comme
la neige, fera la roue autour de l'inaudible.

¶

Nous ne sommes pas un auteur, mais un promeneur
désemparé.
L'effusion de la phrase ne nous est point
spontanée, et nous avons
peu de goût pour les images ensorcelantes.
Notre plainte
est un interminable glas qui sonne l'absence
de langage.
Quelle que soit sa grandeur,
la vérité qui vient d'un livre est une abomination.

¶

The noise
made by the snow renders barely perceptible
the fragment of being
which falls and thinks itself a fragment
of snow.
It would take a soft and bending ear
to convert
that lightness into an experience of the world.
Once again, my words, like
the snow, will fan out around the unheard.

¶

I am not an author, but a directionless
stroller.
The effusion of the word is not
spontaneous in me, and I have
little taste for spellbinding images.
My complaint
is an endless knell which tolls the absence
of language.
Whatever its grandeur,
book truth is horrific.

¶

Le froid consumait les moineaux. Lente, leur
respiration semblait archaïque.
Au centre
de leur rigidité brillait une flamme que l'hiver
alimentait de fagots de neige.
Dans la nuit
resplendissante de tous les frimas,
leur duvet
était gonflé comme des taies d'oxygène.
En fait, ils étaient immolés à la blancheur.

¶

Depuis que le gel s'est installé au verger,
les dernières pommes
sont gagnées par la fadeur du plâtre.
Elles sont touchées
par une discrète circoncision de la saveur.
Elles ne sont plus que des fruits pour
des palais funéraires.
La pauvreté de leur goût
nous rappelle notre âme lorsque celle-ci savoure
sa profondeur exsangue.

¶

Cold consumed the sparrows. Slow, their
breathing seemed archaic.
In the middle
of their stiffness burned a flame which the winter
fed with bundles of snow.
In the night
shining with all the hoarfrost,
their down
was swollen like airbags.
In fact, they were immolated by whiteness.

¶

Since the frost gripped the orchard,
the last apples
have been overtaken by the blandness of plaster.
They are touched
by a discreet circumcision of flavour.
They are no more than fruits for
funerary palates.
The poverty of their taste
reminds us of our soul when it savours
its bloodless depth.

¶

J'ai dû rassembler ma propre immensité pour tenir
tête à la neige.
Sa pâleur
ressemblait au système du néant vu à travers
le sommeil.
Jusqu'ici
j'avais vécu dans une encoignure ; je me sentais
peu fondé à dire «il n'y a rien».
La voyant si blanche, je voulais
être digne de son enchantement sans emploi.

¶

Je n'atteins plus le monde comme d'aucuns
n'aiment pas de dormir.
Je ne m'enivre plus de l'ambition héroïque
de dépouiller
l'horizon de ses richesses.
Je savais qu'il est un itinéraire des curiosités
qu'on ne visite pas,
un guide
qui explique le parcours de ce qui n'est point.
J'ai enduré les pires privations
pour m'assurer de n'arriver nulle part.

¶

I have had to muster my own immensity
to face the snow.
Its pallor
resembled the system of nothingness seen through
sleep.
Until now
I had lived in corners; I felt
no grounds to say "there is nothing".
Seeing it so white, I wanted
to be worthy of its useless spell.

¶

I do not connect with the world anymore just as others
do not like to sleep.
I no longer grow elated by the heroic ambition
of stripping
the horizon of its riches.
I knew it to be a route of oddities
which you do not visit,
a guide
which explains the way of what is not.
I have endured the worst privations
to ensure that I get nowhere.

¶

Il ne suffit pas de dormir. Il faut encore dépasser
le sommeil qui pense.
Notre repos soulève autant d'arrière-pensées
qu'une parole manquée.
On ne peut pas inviter l'infini
à nous suivre
dans cette hibernation quotidienne rongée de
truismes.
Il faut fermer les yeux pour savoir
que la nuit est un lapsus.

¶

La fin du jour avait cette perfection que l'on
admire
dans un feu qui meurt. Elle nous
faisait découvrir l'art de se déposséder.
Déçue,
la lumière s'entassait sur le bord des fenêtres
et ajoutait
une frange à notre propre
crépuscule.
Notre rien s'épaississait à vue d'œil.

¶

It is not enough to sleep. We even have to get past
the sleep which thinks.
Our rest stirs as many thoughts in the back of the mind
as do wasted words.
We cannot invite the infinite
to follow us
into that daily hibernation eaten away by
truisms.
We have to close our eyes to know
the night as a slip of the tongue.

¶

Day's end had that perfection which we
admire
in a dying fire. It made us
discover the art of self-dispossession.
Disillusioned,
the light piled up on the window ledge
and added
a fringe to our own
twilight.
Our nothingness grew thicker before our eyes.

¶

Que serait ce triomphe dont parlent
les sens ?
Que serait cette abondance de grâces qu'on nous
promet au plus profond de nos plaisirs?
Rien!
Le corps
est calqué sur ce qui ne pèse rien.
L'être
est une réprobation qui se tient autant
dans nos signes que dans nos convulsions.

¶

Au début du soir, lorsqu'on regarde
par-dessus la balustrade de nos souvenirs,
nous remarquons
que notre personne s'éloigne, cette personne
qui faisait autrefois nos délices.
Paradoxalement,
On n'est point fâché de se voir disparaître.
Il ne nous plaît pas d'avoir été jeté
dans la fausse singularité de l'individu.
Le moi, c'était la claque de notre conscience!

¶

What would be that triumph of which the senses
speak?
What would be those abundant favours
promised to us in our deepest bliss?
Nothing!
The body
is traced on what has no weight.
Being
is a disapproval which holds as true
in our signs as in our convulsions.

¶

In early evening, when we look
over the balustrade of our memories,
we notice
that our person grows remote, that person
who once delighted us.
Paradoxically,
we are not at all vexed to see ourselves disappear.
We are not pleased to have been thrown
into the false singularity of the individual.
The self, it was the smack of our conscience!

BIOGRAPHICAL NOTES

FRANÇOIS JACQMIN, acknowledged as one of the foremost francophone Belgian poets of the latter half of the twentieth century, was born in 1929 in Horion-Hozémont in the province of Liège. In 1940 his family fled to England to escape the German occupation. He learned English in a school run by Spanish Jesuits, discovered English literature, and wrote his first unpublished poems in English. He returned to Belgium in 1948 and rediscovered his native language and literature. His association with the irreverent, experimental group that formed around the magazine *Phantomas* inspired him to develop a distinctive identity as a poet inspired by art, nature, philosophy, and psychoanalysis. His three major volumes of poetry are *Les Saisons* (1979), *Le Domino gris* (1984), and *Le Livre de la neige* (1990). *Eléments de géométrie*, a volume of prose poems written a few years before his death in 1992, was published in 2005.

PHILIP MOSLEY is Professor of English and Comparative Literature at Pennsylvania State University. He earned his M.A. in European literature and his Ph.D. in comparative literature from the University of East Anglia. Among his book publications are *Split Screen: Belgian Cinema and Cultural Identity*, *Ingmar Bergman: The Cinema as Mistress*, and *Georges Rodenbach: Critical Essays*. He has translated *The Intelligence of Flowers* by Maurice Maeterlinck, *Bruges-la-Morte* by Georges Rodenbach, *Tea Masters, Teahouses* by Werner Lambersy, and *October Long Sunday* by Guy Vaes. In 2008 he was awarded the Prix de la Traduction Littéraire by the French Community of Belgium for his translations of Belgian authors into English.

CLIVE SCOTT is Professor Emeritus of European Literature at the University of East Anglia. His principal research interests lie in French and comparative poetics (*The Poetics of French Verse: Studies in Reading*, 1998; *Channel Crossings: French and English Poetry in Dialogue 1550-2000*, 2002 [awarded the R.H. Gapper Book Prize, 2004]); in literary translation, and in particular the translation of poetry (*Translating Baudelaire*, 2000; *Translating Rimbaud's 'Illuminations'*, 2006); and in photography's relationship with writing (*The Spoken Image: Photography and Language*, 1999; *Street Photography: From Atget to Cartier-Bresson*, 2007). He is at present working on a book on the translation of Apollinaire's poetry. He was elected a Fellow of the British Academy in 1994.

Also available in the Arc Publications
'VISIBLE POETS' SERIES (Series Editor: Jean Boase-Beier)

No. 1
MIKLÓS RADNÓTI (Hungary)
Camp Notebook
Translated by Francis Jones, introduced by George Szirtes

No. 2
BARTOLO CATTAFI (Italy)
Anthracite
Translated by Brian Cole, introduced by Peter Dale
(Poetry Book Society Recommended Translation)

No. 3
MICHAEL STRUNGE (Denmark)
A Virgin from a Chilly Decade
Translated by Bente Elsworth, introduced by John Fletcher

No. 4
TADEUSZ RÓZEWICZ (Poland)
recycling
Translated by Barbara Bogoczek (Plebanek) & Tony Howard,
introduced by Adam Czerniawski

No. 5
CLAUDE DE BURINE (France)
Words Have Frozen Over
Translated by Martin Sorrell, introduced by Susan Wicks

No. 6
CEVAT ÇAPAN (Turkey)
Where Are You, Susie Petschek?
Translated by Cevat Çapan & Michael Hulse,
introduced by A. S. Byatt

No. 7
JEAN CASSOU (France)
33 Sonnets of the Resistance
With an original introduction by Louis Aragon
Translated by Timothy Adès, introduced by Alistair Elliot

No. 8
ARJEN DUINKER (Holland)
The Sublime Song of a Maybe
Translated by Willem Groenewegen, introduced by Jeffrey Wainwright

No. 9
MILA HAUGOVÁ (Slovakia)
Scent of the Unseen
Translated by James & Viera Sutherland-Smith,
introduced by Fiona Sampson

No. 10
ERNST MEISTER (Germany)
Between Nothing and Nothing
Translated by Jean Boase-Beier, introduced by John Hartley Williams

No. 11
YANNIS KONDOS (Greece)
Absurd Athlete
Translated by David Connolly, introduced by David Constantine

No. 12
BEJAN MATUR (Turkey)
In the Temple of a Patient God
Translated by Ruth Christie, introduced by Maureen Freely

No. 13
GABRIEL FERRATER (Catalonia / Spain)
Women and Days
Translated by Arthur Terry, introduced by Seamus Heaney

No. 14
INNA LISNIANSKAYA (Russia)
Far from Sodom
Translated by Daniel Weissbort, introduced by Elaine Feinstein

No. 15
SABINE LANGE (Germany)
The Fishermen Sleep
Translated by Jenny Williams, introduced by Mary O'Donnell

No. 16
TAKAHASHI MUTSUO (Japan)
We of Zipangu
Translated by James Kirkup & Tamaki Makoto, introduced by Glyn Pursglove

No. 17
JURIS KRONBERGS (Latvia)
Wolf One-Eye
Translated by Mara Rozitis, introduced by Jaan Kaplinski

No. 18
REMCO CAMPERT (Holland)
I Dreamed in the Cities at Night
Translated by Donald Gardner, introduced by Paul Vincent

No. 19
DOROTHEA ROSA HERLIANY (Indonesia)
Kill the Radio
Translated by Harry Aveling, introduced by Linda France

No. 20
SOLEIMAN ADEL GUÉMAR (Algeria)
State of Emergency
Translated by Tom Cheesman & John Goodby, introduced by Lisa Appignanesi
(PEN Translation Award)

No. 21
ELI TOLARETXIPI (Spain / Basque)
Still Life with Loops
Translated by Philip Jenkins, introduced by Robert Crawford

No. 22
FERNANDO KOFMAN (Argentina)
The Flights of Zarza
Translated by Ian Taylor, introduced by Andrew Graham Yooll

No. 23
LARISSA MILLER (Russia)
Guests of Eternity
Translated by Richard McKane, introduced by Sasha Dugdale
(Poetry Book Society Recommended Translation)

No. 24
ANISE KOLTZ (Luxembourg)
At the Edge of Night
Translated by Anne-Marie Glasheen, introduced by Caroline Price

No. 25
MAURICE CAREME (Belgium)
Defying Fate
Translated by Christopher Pilling, introduced by Martin Sorrell

No. 26
VALÉRIE ROUZEAU (France)
Cold Spring in Winter
Translated by Susan Wicks, introduced by Stephen Romer

No. 27
RAZMIK DAVOYAN (France)
Whispers and Breath of the Meadows
Translated by Arminé Tamrazian, introduced by W. N. Herbert